CW01658925

PENTLAND WALKS

 7165

Published by: JOHN BARTHOLOMEW & SON LIMITED
DUNCAN STREET, EDINBURGH EH9 1TA

Printed by: K. & R. DAVIDSON LIMITED
207 WEST GEORGE STREET, GLASGOW G2 2LS

ISBN: 07028 0150 X

PENTLAND WALKS

Their literary and historical associations

By D. G. Moir

John Bartholomew & Son Ltd.
Duncan Street
Edinburgh
EH9 ITA

IN PENTLAND WINE

BY

WILL H. OGILVIE

Up here with the wind in our faces,
And the brown heath under our feet,
We look through the shimmering spaces
Over tower and steeple and street
To the Lion splendidly sleeping,
To the tall Crags silent and grey,
To the Castle its grim guard keeping,
And the shining shield of the Bay.

Behind us the mists of the valley
Lie low on the moorland's breast,
With the bonnie banks of Bonaly
In the grey of the winter dressed.
The west wind, wanton, is chiding
Glencorse with the scourge of his whips,
And the wild ducks over it riding
Are tossing like storm-tossed ships.

Up here with the clean winds blowing,
I look to you, City of mine,
I fill me a goblet o'erflowing
And pledge you in Pentland wine!
With a full heart thrilled by your story,
While the hills stand round like kings,
I drink to your lasting glory
In the wine that the hill-wind brings!

Reminiscent of a walk with the poet, from Bonaly to Glencorse, by Castlelaw, and Easter Howgate to Edinburgh.—R.C.

CONTENTS

From Halkerside, from topmost Allermuir
Or steep Caerketton, dreaming, gaze again.

ROBERT LOUIS STEVENSON.

Acknowledgments

Grateful acknowledgment is made of the financial assistance from Lothian Regional Council which has helped to make this publication possible and for the individual contributions made by officials of the Recreation and Leisure Department.

Acknowledgment is also made of the indebtedness to the original publication "Pentland Walks", by Robert Cochrane, published in 1908, from which considerable material has been taken in compiling the present volume.

D.G.M.

A companion to this publication is the "Pentland Hills" map of John Bartholomew & Son Ltd., on the scale of 1½ inches to 1 mile.

The map on page 8 is part of the map of the Lothians by Timothy Pont, which appears in the Gerard Mercator Atlas of 1660. A facsimile reproduction of this map is published by John Bartholomew & Son Ltd.

The Country Code

Guard against all risks of fire.
Fasten all gates.
Keep dogs under proper control.
Keep to the paths across farmland.
Avoid damaging fences, hedges and walls.
Leave no litter.
Safeguard water supplies.
Protect wildlife, wild plants and trees.
Go carefully on country roads.
Respect the life of the Countryside.

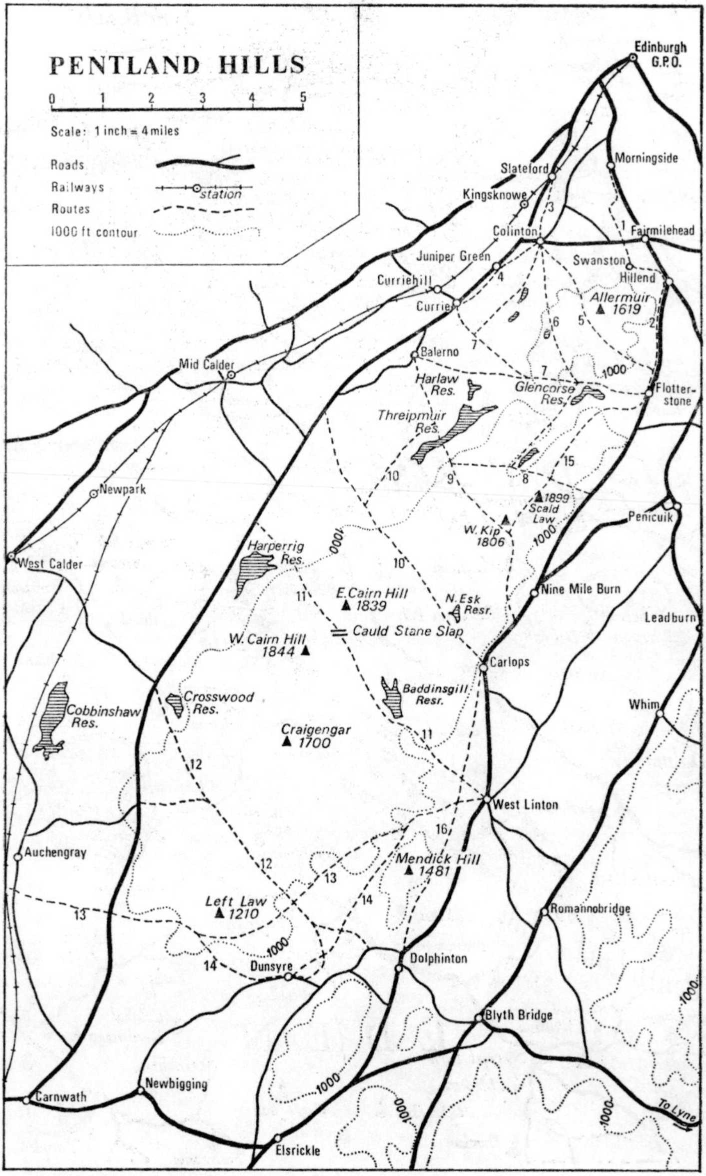
PENTLAND HILLS
0 1 2 3 4 5
Scale: 1 inch = 4 miles
Roads
Railways
station
Routes
1000 ft contour
Edinburgh G.P.O.
Morningside
Slateford
Kingsknowe
Colinton
Fairmilehead
Juniper Green
Swanston
Hillend
Curriehill
Currie
Allermuir 1619
Balerno
Mid Calder
Harlaw Res.
Glencorse Res.
Flotterstone
Threipmuir Res.
Newpark
1899
Scald Law
W. Kip 1806
Penicuik
West Calder
Harperrig Res.
Nine Mile Burn
E. Cairn Hill 1839
N. Esk Resr.
Leadburn
Cauld Stane Slap
W. Cairn Hill 1844
Carlops
Crosswood Res.
Baddinsgill Resr.
Whim
Cobbinshaw Res.
Craigengar 1700
West Linton
Auchengray
Mendick Hill 1481
Left Law 1210
Romannobridge
Dunsyre
Dolphinton
Blyth Bridge
Newbigging
Carnwath
Elsrickle
To Lyne

Lyth Roade
Dolphingtoun
Mainshou
Burnshot
Kattmoore
Kragy
East Kragy
Kragy hal
Pilridge
Bridgs end
Grantoun
Nether Kramont
Wardy
Newhaven
Laurencetoun
Nether Bartoun
Moore hous
Pilmuse
Bonitoun
Lyth
Restalrig
Over Kramont
W. Dryley
E. Dryley
over Barntoun
Kaerlaury
Nether Lany
Kannock
Inner Lyth
Tilrig
Broughtoun
Over Lany
Southfield
Gracruik
Revelstoun
Kraig
Silver mill
E. Craigs
Briggs
Needowfied
Coldham
Hill
Haus
Halyards
West craigs
Korstorphin
Newbridge
Darry m
Holirudhous
Edenburgh
Korstor. C.
Sauchtoun
Marchistnen
East field
Nether Gogar
Gogar mil
Gorgy
Sauchtoun
Craighous
Grange
Brome house
Lochna Burn
Gorgymill
Rathowbyres
Hermistoun
Rydhewes
Loch end
E. Hales
Kray
Rydd hall
H
Y
R
E
F
Dalbertoun
Over Braid
Oxtoun
Wester Hales
Adestoun
Ricartoun
Keyrhill
Burn house
Colintoun
Woodhall
Dalmahay
Coldheun
Mortoun hall
Mortoun
Wauistoun
Bonely
Over Curry
Curry
Stratoun
Stratoun
Killyth
Curry hill
Hiland
Estertoun
Dalmahoy
Lumphoy
Pentland hill
Lyips
Penthland
Pilmoore
Quilridge
Byrney
Harelaw
Loganes
Roslyin more
O
F
Catharins
Paradise
Wholpsyid
Colcburn
Dalmahay crags
Glen crose
Castelaw
Colledge
N. house
Brucley
Achindinny
Roslyin
Butlonds
Gartsyid Kirk
Miltoun
Greenlaw
Woodhousley
Huse in the moor
Pennycook
Woolhousley
Karkettill
Achindynny
Butlond hill
Cotts
Lukenes
Overyrsyit
hill
Skewin den
Penth-land
Brounstoun
Ravensneuck
Cotts
Fatlipps
Karingtoun
Halles
Surnelstoups
Broudwood
Welstoun
Coldhal
Karingtoun barnes
E
D
E
N
Foir Spittel
Nyrmyl burn
Headstone
Achincork
New hall
Mosshouse
Kings seat
Harelaw
Temple
Freere toun

Introductory

Area of the Pentlands—Scott and Stevenson—Land Use—Access —How to reach the Pentlands—Pentland Hills Ranger Service.

WITH or without company, a hill-walk is one of the good things of this life which inspire towards what is best in nature and human nature. Provided the ground be dry, such a walk is as good in winter as in summer. Dwellers in Edinburgh especially, and rural Midlothian, are fortunate in having the "Pentlands' long line softening into blue" close at hand, "like a wedge of wild nature and old romance thrust into the heart of a workaday world." No road crosses them throughout their length, and sometimes to the tired pedestrian the bus routes seem to keep a too respectful distance. Pentland memories are of many kinds, homely and heroic, literary and historic, humorous and tragic, and here we recall the more interesting and important of them.

AREA OF THE PENTLANDS

The eastern and Edinburgh end of the Pentland range is best known, and has been more glorified by poets and litterateurs than where the western slopes sink gently towards the Clyde valley. Their undulating blue lines are so homelike to the returning wanderer, and in parting seem to say, "I will haunt you: you will never forget me".

The name is believed to have been derived from Petland or Pictland. On the east this fine range starts on the south-west of Edinburgh and extends westwards through the counties of Midlothian, Peebles, and Lanark, for about sixteen miles to near Carnwath, where it slopes into Clydesdale. Its average breadth is from four to six miles, broken up by fine ravines and hollows, the principal pass being the Cauldstane Slap between West Linton and Mid Calder, passing between East Cairn and West Cairn Hills. The highest points are Carnethy (1890 feet) and Scald Law (1899 feet), which rise from the old Biggar Road, nine miles south-west from Edinburgh.

The range embraces within its areas the peak, the precipice, and the rounded or broad-shouldered hills, forming valleys, the birthplace of many streams, affording delightful walks happily available to the pedestrian who may choose, as befits his walking powers, between the five-mile route from Colinton to Glencorse, or the eight-mile one between the Lanark road and West Linton, enjoying in varied directions views of river, strath and wood; the Forth, the Ochils and the Grampians; not least that of "mine own romantic town".

Sir Walter Scott, with his unerring eye for the picturesque and wonderful descriptive power, after a drive at sunset between Lasswade and Edinburgh, wrote: "I think I never saw anything more beautiful than the ridge of Carnethy against a clear frosty sky, with its peaks and varied slopes. The hills glowed like purple amethyst; the sky glowed topaz and vermilion colours. I never saw a finer series than Pentlands considering that it is neither rocky nor highly elevated". To Lord Cockburn the competitors for the first prize amongst hills were only Ben Lomond, Dumyat, and Caerketton, above Swanston. He balanced the claims of each, and his judicial mind, considering the beauty of Edinburgh and the dignity imparted to scenery by objects of importance, was inclined to give the palm to Pentlands. The fact that R. L. Stevenson lived when a lad with his father and mother in the hamlet of Swanston, below Caerketton, accounts for the sketches of the shepherd and the garden in his *Memories and Portraits*, the delightful description in *Edinburgh: Picturesque Notes*, and many references in his letters and some of his stories, such as *St. Ives*. He remembered the spot, above the Shearers' Knowe at Swanston, whence the nameless trickle to supply the water-filters comes, where he sat and made bad verses. The Pentlands, said John Geddie, may lay claim to be the birthplace of the genius of R. L. Stevenson; they were his study and classroom, and at Swanston he believes the awakening took place.

James Ballantine tries to express in verse the sights and sounds of a summer day on the hills:—

Those airy tones that lightly float
Seem bursting from the linnet's throat;
Anon, afar the shy cuckoo
Soothes with his strain the lone curlew;
The grasshopper, with elfin drum,
Beats time unto the wild bee's hum;
And, with a low sweet music fills
Each fairy nook of Pentland Hills.

But, lo! the cadence louder swells—
The chimes of fair Edina's bells,
Far in the distance, wake the ear;
Anon they burst in fulness near,
And o'er grey crag and valley green,
Each tiny leaf is dancing seen,
And every streamlet gurgling trills
In joy amid the Pentland Hills.

Land Use

Although the hills seem to the pedestrian to be designed for a recreational area, the major use is in fact for farming, with a small amount of forestry and some subsidiary uses. Sheep farming is predominant, principally Blackface flocks, with more sheep to the acre than is the average throughout Scotland. Where farms have low ground fields, as well as hill grazings, the lambs can be kept and fattened on the lower pastures; otherwise they are sold. Some of the hill farms are now being given over more to the grazing of beef cattle. Afforestation is so far little in evidence, but recently the Forestry Commission planted ground south of Harperrig Reservoir, and there has been private planting at Baddinsgill. On the lower ground are numerous shelter belts for protection of fields or farm steadings from the cold blasts. Nearly a twentieth of the land surface is used for agricultural research in the Easter Howgate—Flotterstone area. Thirteen reservoirs either supply water for Edinburgh—one tenth of the city's needs—or serve as compensation reservoirs to maintain a steady supply to mills on the various streams. The military have a training area, at the north-eastern end, and the public have recreational parks at Bonaly and Hillend.

Access

All the routes described in this book, except Route 5 (Howden Glen to Castle Law) are rights of way over which the public have unrestricted passage; and on Route 5, which is over land in military occupation, walkers are permitted when the firing range is not in use. Apart from the rights of way you are on private ground but it is the general experience that walkers are allowed to go anywhere on the hills provided they do not disturb sheep (especially in the lambing season in the Spring), or cattle, and give a wide berth to any party out shooting.

For the nearer routes, those starting from Colinton, Currie, Balerno, or Midcalder, no special equipment is required beyond a stout pair of shoes or boots and some protection against rain. The map is always useful and certainly for the more distant routes the map is essential, and also a compass except in the most settled weather conditions.

Distances are given in miles. In reckoning time the usual rule is to allow an hour for every three miles for a steady pace, plus half an hour extra for the climb in crossing the hills. This applies to the easier routes where there is a path; on the more distant routes where much of the way is through heather or tussocky grass allow more time. In any case allow longer if you are slow on the hills or not a good walker.

The signposts on the various routes have been provided by the Scottish Rights of Way Society, some of them as far back as 1885. The Society welcomes new members: apply to the Secretary at 28 Rutland Square, Edinburgh, EH1 2BW, for membership.

How to reach the Pentlands

We give here a good deal of material about the skirts of the Pentlands. For those who wish to get upon the hills at once, city buses run to Fairmilehead (in summer to Hillend), Colinton, and Juniper Green; buses of Eastern Scottish run to Balerno, Mid Calder, West Calder, and (morning only) to Auchengray, on the north side of the Pentlands, and on the south side to Flotterstone, Glencorse, Penicuik, Nine Mile Burn, Carlops, West Linton, Dolphinton, and Dunsyre. Mid Calder and West Calder are also served by trains.

There are inns or tea-rooms at Colinton, Juniper Green, Currie, Balerno and Mid Calder on the north side; at Flotterstone, Penicuik, Nine Mile Burn, Carlops, West Linton and Dolphinton on the south.

Pentland Hills Ranger Service

The Regional Council, with the advice and financial assistance of the Countryside Commission for Scotland, has formed a Ranger Service. The Rangers will help the area and visitors by advising, guiding and informing them about the hills and the many interests to be seen and enjoyed. At the same time the Service will keep the Countryside Code firmly in front of all who use the hills so that all will develop the 'good manners' which will assist, rather than hinder, the work of the farmers and other principal users.

Footpath repairs and other 'odd-jobs' will be carried out, and the Rangers are available, during the quieter part of the year, to visit and lecture at schools or other organisations.

From the small Countryside Centre at Hillend, (031-445 3383) you may have further information about the Pentlands, especially the Countryside Parks of Hillend and Bonaly.

I. Route I—To Swanston and Caerketton by Morningside — 3 to 4 Miles

Hermitage of Braid—Scott and Burns on the Braids—The Buck Stone—Morton Hall—Cromwell's Camp—Greenbank and Comiston—Hunter's Tryst—Swanston—Association with Stevenson—Swanston Cottage—View from Caerketton.

An easily accomplished Pentland ramble is that to Swanston, the tiny hamlet associated with R. L. Stevenson, nestling at the north base of Caerketton, and consisting of a farmhouse, Swanston Cottage and a few cottages. For this route there is the bus for those who wish it to Fairmilehead, but the walk, either from the former Morningside Station by the old Braid Road or from Greenbank through Braidburn Valley by the footpath, provides much of interest.

R.L.S. in the chapter "To the Pentland Hills" in his *Edinburgh—Picturesque Notes* describes the walk by road up to Fairmilehead as "a long hot walk in summer time". He tells us that when a child he used to be shown a flat stone in the roadway to which the gibbet had been fixed when two men were hanged in January 1815 for robbing the Biggar carrier at that spot. Two stones may still be seen in Braid Road opposite Comiston Terrace. This was the last instance in Scotland of hanging for highway robbery.

Hermitage of Braid

Sir William Dick of Braid was Lord Provost of Edinburgh in 1638–39, and a zealous Covenanter. He became owner of the Braid estate in 1631 by purchase from Sir Robert Fairlie. It was then divided into Upper and Lower Braid, including Mains of Braid, with the Manor Place, Briggs of Braid, and Braid Craig (Hills), Blackford, Greenbank, Plewlands, Smiddigreen and Egypt Farm, with the cottages and crofts on the same. Charles Gordon of Cluny, bought the Braid estate about 1771 and built the present mansion, the Hermitage. He died in 1814, and later Gordons of Cluny have continued in the ownership of the estate.

Sir John Skelton, the apologist for Queen Mary and biographer of Lethington, lived and wrote and died at Hermitage. Sir John has left memorials of some of the noted people, such as J. A. Froude, Professor Blackie, Jowett, Huxley, Sellar, Sir Noel Paton and others, who visited the Hermitage.

The Hermitage of Braid and grounds now belong to the city; the ground are open to the public.

Scott and Burns on the Braids

Scott's fine lines on Edinburgh from the Braids are well known. One would fain believe that when Burns was having an early morning stroll with Dugald Stewart on the Braids, it was a distant prospect of some smoking cottages which gave such pleasure to his mind, a pleasure he said none could understand who had not witnessed the like himself, because of the happiness and worth they contained. And no doubt the walk with Painter Nasmyth to the Pentlands, straight from a High Street tavern, at 3 a.m., was by this route. It was then that the poet was frightened by a lunatic in a cottage. They came down from the hills to Roslin for breakfast.

The Buck Stone

The old road descends to the Braid Burn at Hermitage Gate and passes the lodge built of the stones of the old Morningside Toll Bar, and an exact facsimile. As we go southward we pass Braid Hills Road, and on the left hand, beyond the Mortonhall Golf Club House, the rock known as the "Buck Stone", a large fragment, on which the proprietor of the Barony of Penicuik is bound by his tenure to sit and wind three blasts of a horn when the King shall come to hunt on the Borough Muir. Hence the crest of the Clerks of Penicuik—a demi-forester proper, winding a horn, with the motto, "Frie for a blast". Scott gives this tradition in a note to his *Gray Brother*. Maitland, in his *History of Edinburgh*, relates this regarding the Bore Stone near Church Hill, and the Buck Stone, he says, was thus named because the King's buck-hounds were unchained here. Some stone cists were found on the highest point of the Braids about the middle of last century.

Morton Hall — Cromwell's Camp

At Fairmilehead four roads meet. That to the east leads to Morton House, where John Hill Burton, the historian, died in 1881. Morton House, like Morton Hall, which lies further east, belonged, in James III's time, to Sir Oliver Sinclair of Roslin; the estate at that period was attached to the Barony of Pentland. The founder of the Trotter family of Mortonhall was John Trotter, a benevolent Edinburgh merchant, who sprang from a Berwickshire family. Galachlaw, the southward-sloping ridge from the Braids, between Mortonhall on the east and Fairmilehead on the west, is the place (just behind the Princess Margaret Rose Hospital) where Cromwell encamped before the battle of Dunbar. The month of August 1650 was exceptionally wet, and some 2000 of his troops were on the sick list. "Blessed be God", ran a sentence in a letter next year, "we have now other shelter and footing than Pentland Hills", which was the name given by the soldiers to the Braids, Blackford, Craiglockhart and Colinton neighbourhood. There was no timber here at that time: they had to erect a gallows for a sergeant who had looted a cloak, but "there was no tree to hang him on". In the summer of 1651 Cromwell and his Ironsides were again stationed "towards Colingtoun" on Pentland Hills ("our old quarters"). Colonel Lilburne wrote to Cromwell that the soldiers "eate biskett and cheese on Pentland Hills".

Moving westwards along Oxgangs Road we see on the right, in a recess in Caiystane View, a monolith of red sandstone, 9 ft. 3 inches high, supposed to mark the scene of an ancient battle, as, when the road along which we are passing was formed, many stone cists were found, with skeletons within them. It is known as the Caiy Stane, or battle-stone. The Camus Stone has disappeared from this neighbourhood, as have also two other conical cairns.

Greenbank and Comiston

The alternative route from Morningside by Greenbank comes in at the next street on the right, Caiystane Drive. The path up the Braidburn Valley enters the park at Greenbank Crescent between two stone pillars, once forming the gateway of Comiston House, which were erected here when the valley was acquired for a public park in 1937. The Braid Burn is followed to the far end of the park, where the bridge is crossed to reach the path seen going uphill past Comiston cistern, to which the water is led from the various Comiston springs. From these springs came an early water supply for Edinburgh. Peter Bruschi, a Dutchman, was paid about £3000 in 1681 for laying a lead pipe, 3 inches in diameter, from Comiston to the reservoir on Castle Hill. This pipe was twice replaced by larger ones, and the supply still being insufficient for the expanding city, a pipe was laid in 1761 to bring water from the springs at Swanston, at first wooden pipes, replaced in 1790 by an iron pipe of 7 inches diameter. The next step was a reservoir at Bonaly and in 1819 a company was formed to bring water from Crawley Springs near Flotterstone. The Comiston water is no longer used in the city because of the local housing developments, and now flows into the Braid Burn. The filters on the east of the road at Fairmilehead deal with the water brought by pipes from Talla Reservoir in the hills above the Upper Tweed.

The path passes a farmhouse, all that remains of Comiston Farm, and then goes alongside the trees sheltering Comiston House (now Caiystane Park Hotel), a mansion built in 1815 by James Forrest, whose son, Sir James, was Lord Provost of Edinburgh, 1837–43.

Hunter's Tryst

On reaching Oxgangs Road the road to Swanston is facing us, but first we should note on the right the buildings at the bend in the road known as Hunter's Tryst. This was once a howff of the Six Foot Club, of which Scott and Hogg were members. It continued as an inn up to 1862, then became a farm and dairy, and now has reverted to its original purpose of serving food and drink but in a more elegant style. There is a scene in *St. Ives* located here by Stevenson. On a clear day, from hereabouts the hills of Fife, the Ochils and Ben Ledi, stand out against the northern sky. The road passing by the left of Hunter's Tryst leads alongside the woods of Dreghorn to Dreghorn Loan at Colinton and just beyond Dreghorn Mains to a track leading over to Bonaly Public Park.

Swanston

We now take the road going south to Swanston, and see before us the ruddy screes of Caerketton, with the modern ski lift, and the T-shaped wood, then lower down the cluster of trees which shelter the picturesque hamlet of Swanston. To the right of this is Swanston Cottage, leased by R. L. Stevenson's father from 1867 to 1880, where the family spent a large part of their summers. These summers at Swanston left abiding impressions on R.L.S. which are reflected in much of his writings. The farm, he says in *Picturesque Notes*, had an open door during Covenanting times when a night conventicle was held on the Pentlands; the dresser was laden with cheese, bannocks, milk and brandy for the worshippers coming down from the hill. There is a memorial to Stevenson in St. Giles Cathedral; a monument-fountain has been erected to his memory in San Francisco; a fountain might well be erected to his memory at Swanston, now quite a place of pilgrimage.

Associations with Stevenson

Sir John Skelton mentions having walked over from Hermitage of Braid to Swanston Cottage with Principal Tulloch, to dine with the Stevensons. R.L.S., then only a lad, was absent; but his mother, who treasured every scrap of his writing, gave the two visitors away some juvenile contributions to local journals. Both agreed that here was a fresh voice, with a note delicate and unborrowed as the lark's. Skelton was not sure if he ever did anything better than some of these early trifles.

After the *Pentland Rising* booklet of 1866, the literary fruitage of R. L. Stevenson's life, before he became a fixture at Vailima in Samoa, was shed at all sorts of places. He had also seen all kinds of life. In the days of what he calls his green-sickness, in the sanded kitchen of an Edinburgh public house, he had met seamen, chimney-sweeps and thieves. Once he wrote to his mother: "I must be a bit of a vagabond: it's your own fault after all, isn't it? You shouldn't have had a tramp for a son". By 1886 he had slept in forty-six English towns, fifty in Scotland, seventy-four in France, and forty in the rest of Europe. But the fancy and imagination of R. L. Stevenson continued to hover over well remembered scenes in Edinburgh, Swanston and the Pentlands to the very last; and many of his letters, when any of his old haunts are alluded to, seem to end in a longing sigh, as in some of the last lines he wrote:

I gang nae mair where once I gaed,
By Buckstone, Fairmilehead, or Braid,
But far frae Kirk and Tron.
Oh, still, ayont the muckle sea,
Still are ye dear, and dear to me,
Auld Reekie, still and on.

"It is a singular thing", he writes, "that I should live here in the South Seas, under conditions so new and so striking, and yet my imagination so continually inhabits the cold old huddle of grey hills from which we came". The three fine verses Crockett received in acknowledgment of the dedication of the *Stickit Minister* to the Exile of Samoa, beginning, "Blows the wind to-day," breathe the same feeling. And from far Samoa he wrote:

The tropics vanish; and meseems that I—
From Halkerside, from topmost Allermuir,
Or steep Caerketton—dreaming, gaze again.

The whole panorama rose up before that "inward eye which is the bliss of solitude". There was the town, like an island in the smoke, cragged, spired, and turreted; new folds of the city glitter on seaward-dropping hills. The Forth gleams beyond, and Fife smokes with scores of towns.

"He was just naething when I kenned him", said the worthy woman in whose "ben" had died John Todd, the "Roaring Shepherd", whose likeness figures in *Memories and Portraits*. The old Scottish Gardener is another Swanston reminiscence, and how lovingly Stevenson describes the place in his *Edinburgh—Picturesque Notes*.

Swanston Cottage

In *St. Ives* his imagination was playing in and around Swanston, whither he leads one of his characters, and gives an idealised description of Swanston Cottage: "A single gable and chimney of the cottage peered over the shoulder of the hill; not far off, and a trifle higher on the mountain, a tall old white-washed farmhouse stood among the trees, beside a falling brook; beyond were rough hills of pasture . . The cottage was a little quaint place of many rough cast gables, and grey roofs. It had something of the air of a rambling infinitesimal cathedral, the body of it rising in the midst two storeys high, with a steep pitched roof, and sending out upon all hands (as it were chapter-houses, chapels, and transepts), one-storeyed and dwarfish projections. To add to this appearance, it was grotesquely decorated with crockets and gargoyles, ravished from some mediaeval church".

The gable and chimney of Swanston Cottage still peer over the shoulder of the hill to the right of the farm buildings; in the small house at the entrance gate Stevenson's nurse, Miss Cunningham, the "Cummy" of the Child's Garden of Verses, lived for a time. The "tall old white-washed farmhouse" among the trees and facing the road is now a dark grey and becoming neglected through the lack of a permanent tenant. The road bends left to go up to Swanston village; here the "White House" was the schoolhouse and the cottage attached to it the school before the last war. Beyond is the picturesque village, with its old thatched cottages facing the village green through which flows the Swanston Burn. At the top of the green a seat has been provided with an inscription "To the memory of Edwin Muir, 1882–1959. Poet, Novelist, Essayist, Teacher. This seat is given by his friends to the village of Swanston where the poet liked to linger and meditate".

View from Caerketton

There is a very extensive and interesting view from the top of Caerketton, just above Swanston. A well-used track goes up by the Swanston Burn to Allermuir; at the head of the burn, where the track bends right, a short but fairly steep climb up by the end of Caerketton Craigs leads to a dip in the ridge, from which it is only a short distance to the summit of Caerketton. An alternative ascent is by the ski lift in Hillend Park. There is a path from Caerketton to the top of Allermuir. The view from the summit is immense; from the base of Caerketton the land falls and swells to the southern shores of the Firth of Forth, its undulations broken by the ridge of Edinburgh City, the Castle Rock, Calton Hill and Arthur's Seat.

Eastward along the Firth are seen North Berwick Law and the Bass Rock; somewhat nearer are the Garleton Hills and Traprain Law. On the south-east horizon the Lammermuirs merge into the Moorfoots; beyond them on a clear day may be seen the top of Cheviot. To the north-west are the Grampians, with Ben Lomond, Ben Vorlich and Ben Ledi being conspicuous; east of them are the round Ochils and the twin summits of the Lomond Hills, and in the more distant north is Dundee Law.

2. Route 2—Swanston to Flotterstone and Glencorse 5 Miles

Hillend—Pentland Churchyard—Memories of the Road—Old and New Woodhouselee—Woodhouselee and the Tytlers—Scott at Woodhouselee—The Highlanders here during the '45—Easter Howgate—Glencorse Old Kirk—R. L. Stevenson's Memories of Glencorse—*Pentland Rising*—Rullion Green Martyrs' Monument—The Rising of 1666—House of Muir—Mauricewood—Penicuik and the Paper Industry—Penicuik Worthies.

A cart road skirts Lothianburn golf course and gives access from Swanston to the Biggar Road. On the south side of Lothianburn is Hillend Park, a splendid stretch of hill slope presented to the town in 1924 as a public recreation ground on the Pentlands. Those who have climbed Caerketton from Swanston can come down through Hillend Park to the main road.

Pentland Churchyard

Past Lothianburn there are three roads from which to choose. The road to Flotterstone ascends to the right but, if time permits, a visit might first be made to the hamlet of Old Pentland which lies a mile to the east along the lowest of the three roads. No trace is left above ground of the ancient church, but in the old graveyard, sheltered by a clump of trees on the left, is the massive vault of the family of Sir John Gibsone of Pentland, who held the barony of Pentland from 1633. Among several old tombstones one marks the grave of Robert Umpherston, tenant in Pentland who died in 1624. The tombstone of Helen Alexander (1654–1729) the heroine of the Scottish Covenanters (and of her husband James Currie), has been taken to Huntly House Museum in Edinburgh. A narrative of her life was published in 1857 with the title of "*A short account of the Lords Dealing with Helen Alexander, spouse first to Charles Umpherston, tenant in Pentland, and thereafter to James Currie, merchant in Pentland*". It is recorded that she was in touch with all the leading Covenanters, she gave help dauntlessly to the fugitives and spent days and nights ministering in prison to the suffering remnant. An inscription on the Martyrs' Monument in Greyfriars churchyard records that "This tomb was first erected by James Curie Mercht in Pentland and others 1706". The old school of the village has a plaque "Erected and Endowed by Mrs. Helen Gibsone 1827".

Returning to Hillend we take the old Biggar Road uphill; though busy with traffic it has a pavement for pedestrians all the way and provides extensive views as it crosses the lower eastern slope of the

Pentland Hills. Here we see eastward the sweep of the Firth of Forth, with the Bass Rock and North Berwick Law. Nearer are Arthur's Seat and the eastern spread of the city; to the south the long range of the Lammermuirs merge into the Moorfoots.

The whole vale of North Esk before us, which Allan Ramsay called the Temple of Scotland, is redolent with memories of celebrities, from near its rise, at North Esk Reservoir above Carlops. At Newhall, Allan Ramsay's "Habbie's Howe" is situated. De Quincey resided for about fifteen years in a cottage known as Mavis Bush, at Polton; then there is Hawthornden, with memories of Drummond; Lasswade, where Scott first set up his household gods after marriage; and near here Mrs. Oliphant records she first awoke to consciousness of things around her. Dalkeith has associations with General Monk, the Buccleuch family, and Norman Macleod. Musselburgh, which was a Roman station, has memories of David Macbeth Moir, poet and author of *Mansie Wauch.*

Memories of the Road

One thinks of the lonely drives of the carrier; the weary coach rides of Thomas Carlyle as a student, by Ericstane and Broughton towards Edinburgh University; or the cheery drives on the Dumfries coach from Princes Street of Christopher North, bent on angling expeditions to Tweedside, beside the Crook, and in Talla Glen. Every Pentland pedestrian thinks of the Covenanters and of the disaster at Rullion Green in 1666, the subject of R. L. Stevenson's virgin booklet. Then Allan Ramsay must have known the Biggar road well, which hugs the south side of the Pentlands.

Alexander Ireland has recorded how scores of times Dr. Hodgson, Dr. Robert Chambers, Robert Cox and himself had crossed the Pentlands from Woodhouselee, by the Compensation Pond, over to Currie. They used to meet at the head of the links, near Morningside, at 7 a.m., and walk out by Lothianburn to Gilchrist's Inn at Woodhouselee, where they always breakfasted. They had the healthy appetites of pedestrians and never, said Ireland, "were there better ham and eggs than those of Mrs. Gilchrist".

Old and New Woodhouselee

After passing Boghall Experimental Farm and Fulford we come to the estate of Woodhouselee. The irregular pile known as Woodhouselee, originally the old fortalice of Fulford, dating from the 14th century, was the residence of the Tytler family from 1748 to 1923. The house owed its name to Sir William Purves of Tofts, who obtained a gift of the Fulford estate, and in 1657 procured a charter from Cromwell erecting the lands of Fulford into a barony. When

Sir William enlarged the tower of Fulford, he brought stones and material for the purpose from the old castle of Woodhouselee, which stands on a bank overlooking the River Esk near Auchendinny, and also transferred the name Woodhouselee to his new property. A ghost clung to the stones of its old habitation, and, as narrated below, gave several generations a lively time. Sir William Purves of Woodhouselee, whose portrait by Lely is in the Scottish National Portrait Gallery, is said by some to have been the original of Sir William Worthy in Allan Ramsay's *Gentle Shepherd.*

We give the commonly accepted tradition regarding Woodhouselee. James Hamilton of Bothwellhaugh had been one of Queen Mary's firmest supporters and fought for her at Langside, where he was made prisoner and sentenced to death. Woodhouselee became the property of Hamilton through his marriage to Lady Anne Sinclair of the Rosslyn family. Regent Moray spared the life of Bothwellhaugh, but forfeited his estates, which he gave to his favourite Ballenden, or Ballantyne, the Justice-Clerk. Bothwellhaugh, thinking that Woodhouselee was not included in the forfeiture, placed his wife there with her infant child and went to join the Earl of Hamilton at Cadzow Castle. Ballenden took the castle of Woodhouselee in his absence, which he burned to the ground. Lady Anne was turned out to the woods with her child where she went mad and perished. It is her ghost with child in arms which has haunted old and new Woodhouselee. Hamilton took vengeance on Regent Moray by shooting him, from a window in Linlithgow, before a year had passed. The higher critics, such as John Hill Burton, have tried to prove that Lady Anne was alive after the death of Regent Moray, and that the real ghost was Lady Anne Bothwell whose lament is well known. It is said, that she and her infant, having been deserted by her husband, returned to Woodhouselee only in time to die. One or other of these stories gave the place the reputation of being haunted. Scott worked the story, as we have said, into his *Cadzow Castle*, where he calls Hamilton's wife Margaret, and in *The Gray Brother* there is the well-known reference to "haunted Woodhouselee" and memories of rambles in the neighbourhood:—

Sweet are the paths, O passing sweet!
By Eske's fair streams that run,
O'er airy steep, through copsewood deep,
Impervious to the sun.

From that fair dome, where suit is paid
By blast of bugle free,
To Auchendinny's hazel glade,
And haunted Woodhouselee.

Woodhouselee and the Tytlers

In 1748 Woodhouselee was bought by William Tytler. The Tytlers were Seatons; how the name was changed and how the founder of the family came across from France in the retinue of Queen Mary is delightfully told, with much else, in the life of Patrick Fraser Tytler, the historian of Scotland, by Dean Burgon. The book is most justly styled *The Portrait of a Christian Gentleman.* William Tytler was widely known for a book defending Queen Mary, and his recipe for a happy old age like his own was, "short but cheerful meals, music, and a good conscience". A new house, incorporating part of the old tower of Fulford, was built in 1796 by William Tytler's son Alexander, who became a judge with the title Lord Woodhouselee. A south wing, added later, was designed and built under the superintendence of G. M. Kemp, architect of the Scott Monument. Lord Woodhouselee, published *Elements of General History*, and succeeded here and at his Princes Street home in gathering round him the most eminent men of his time in his happy household. His translation of Schiller's *Robbers* helped to direct Scott towards German literature. Among his guests, besides Walter Scott, were Professor Dugald Stewart, Lord Jeffrey, Henry Mackenzie, Sydney Smith, Basil Hall, Sir James Stuart of Allanbank, and John Leyden.

Patrick Fraser Tytler, the youngest son of Lord Woodhouselee, took part with Sir Walter Scott in founding the Bannatyne Club, and on Scott's suggestion wrote a history of Scotland, 1249 to 1603, in nine volumes.

In 1936 Woodhouselee house and policies became War Office property and during the war of 1939–45 served as a prisoner of war camp for Germans and Italians. Subsequently the mansion house was demolished.

Scott at Woodhouselee

The great romancer was plain Walter Scott when he haunted Woodhouselee, for he had just set up his household gods in what Miss Tytler thought a poor, dilapidated cottage, with but one good sitting-room, between Lasswade and Loanhead, which may still be seen. On walking over to Scott's cottage at Lasswade one morning, they found him mounted on a ladder nailing together a Gothic arch of willows over the entrance gate. He was very proud of his handiwork and had gone out to admire it in the moonlight on the first night.

Scott was a frequent visitor at Woodhouselee for days at a time when he started housekeeping at Lasswade. After breakfast he commonly proposed a walk, and, says Miss Ann Fraser Tytler, "with his joyous look and vigorous step, he would take his way to what was called the Green Hill of Castlelaw. It was rugged of ascent, but the summer wind as it blew upon us came laden with the fragrance of the wild thyme and purple heather with which it was covered to the very top". They halted at a particular spot, when Scott would start one of his delightful stories, generally the production of his brain at the moment; sometimes he told legends of Covenanters, for there were graves of these men just over Logan Burn at Rullion Green. To these mornings would succeed the evening ghost stories, when the young folks were so excited and spellbound that no one dared move. "How," says Miss Tytler, "could we dare doubt the truth of every word, having ourselves our own legitimate ghost to be believed in?"

At the time of Scott's visits there was one bedroom with a mysterious-looking, small, and very old door, which led into a turret fitted up as a dressing-room. From this small door the ghost was wont to issue. The old nurse when asked about Lady Anne, (the ghost), would say, "Deed, I have seen her times out o' number, but I am in no ways feared. I ken weel she canna gang beyond her commission; but there's that silly, feckless thing Betty, she met her in the lang passage ae nicht in the winter-time, and she hadna a drap o' bluid in her face for a fortnight after. She says Lady Anne came sae near her she could see her dress quite weel; it was a Manchester muslin with a wee flower". Walter Scott used to laugh heartily at this "wee flower", and hoped that Lady Anne would never change her dress.

The Highlanders here during the '45

It is a shock to come suddenly from these gloaming stories to the matter-of-fact laird or tenant of Woodhouselee, who set down all that he knew and saw of the '45 in Edinburgh and his neighbourhood. The diary begins on that Sabbath of 15th September when the worshippers in Glencorse Church were startled by the news that Prince Charlie and his men were marching on Edinburgh. The long sermon by John Wilson and an "ill-timed exhortation", were heard with impatience, and the writer hurried to an eminence of the Pentlands from which the dragoons could be seen at Corstorphine. Next day he saw the cavalcade with the baggage and "Highland wives" pass the Braid Hills towards the camp at Duddingston, and caught a glimpse from Canaan Muir, Morningside, of the Prince and his men on their way to Holyrood.

The Highlanders visited Boghall, Glencorse and Howgate, where they put all Charles Straton's baps and ale on a large fire, and drank whisky. From Woodhouselee they get a little money and bear away the sheets hidden in the hay; from a terrified serving-man hiding in the garden they extract five shillings and sixpence. They retire behind Woodhouselee, quarrel over the booty, march towards Edinburgh, stop a carriage, and then "gulravage" in the public-house at Lothianburn. A fellow captured at Castlelaw has on a fur hat and shirt with cambric ruffles down the breast, very clean, and not bleeding. "No doubt he had robbed the shirt", says the writer.

When Prince Charles was appealed to regarding these depredations by men from Swanston and others, he said if the thieves were pointed out they would be hanged. No more came of it; but the Laird of Woodhouselee no doubt heaved a sigh of relief when with his "prospect glass" he had a clear view of the Highland host, with pipes playing, and replenished in horses, goods and gear, passing on by Milton Bridge to Peebles. "All General Cope's wagons taken at Prestonpans were there. Deserters here and there were picked up; three found on Castlelaw were brought to Woodhouselee; one was wounded by a stone in the head, and all bloody". They were carried forward to Boghall, the next farm, Edinburghwards, and the tables being turned upon them, they were relieved of five guineas and a crown.

Easter Howgate

Beyond Woodhouselee is the pretty hamlet of Easter Howgate, smaller than of yore, and said to have suggested Elizabeth Hamilton's *Cottagers of Glenburnie*, when the authoress was staying at Woodhouselee. On the left, beyond some fields, are the extensive buildings of the Edinburgh Centre of Rural Economy, with headquarters at Bush House, a house built towards the end of the 18th century and subsequently enlarged. At the next farm on the right, Crosshouse, a road goes uphill to Castlelaw Farm and the underground earth house or "souterrain" (see Route 5—key at Crosshouse).

The next road to the left leads to Milton Bridge and Glencorse passing, in the field on the right, the cistern of Crawley springs, from which a pipe was laid to Edinburgh in 1822 to augment the city's supply from Comiston and Swanston. The lands of Glencorse here, in the 17th century, belonged to a family named Bothwell, descended from the Bishop who performed the marriage ceremony between Queen Mary and the Earl of Bothwell. Glencorse House, built about 1812, and Loganbank below Glencorse House, built about 1810, came into the hands of the Dean of the Faculty of Advocates, afterwards Lord President Inglis, in 1855.

Glencorse Old Kirk

Beyond Glencorse House, up a brae on the left, in the wood through which winds Glencorse Burn, are the ruins of the old Church of Glencorse, dating, however, no further back than 1665; having been destroyed by fire in 1695, it was rebuilt in 1699 and enlarged by adding transepts. Above the west door is a panel "Cume let us call upon (Go)d most he (i.e. high). Unto my God that (blank) for me thai thingis for me". At the side are S.W.P., the initials for Sir William Purves of Woodhouselee. The ruins no doubt stand on the site of an older building. When the church was repaired in 1811, an ancient font stone was found below the surface of the floor. After it was deserted in 1885 for the handsome new church close by, it was allowed to become a ruin. Glencross was the old name, possibly from a cross in the valley, or from the hill crossings which start near here.

R. L. Stevenson's Memories of Glencorse

Stevenson thus refers to Glencorse Burn:—"Do you know", he wrote from Samoa to S. R. Crockett, "that the dearest burn to me in the world is that which drums and pours in cunning wimples in that glen of yours behind Glencorse old kirk. Of that I were the lad I once was, sitting under old Torrence, that old shepherd of let-well-alone, and watching with awe the waving of the old black gloves over the Bible—the preacher's white finger-ends meanwhile aspiring through! Man, I would even be willing to sit under you—a sore declension, truly—just to be there". The Mr. Torrence mentioned here left Queen Mary's gold watch to Professor Fraser-Tytler of Woodhouselee and has his name inscribed on a stone in Glencorse churchyard. He died in 1877, aged 89, after 59 years' service. Stevenson thus describes the old church in a note to Sidney Colvin: "It is a little cruciform place, with a steep slate roof. The small kirkyard is full of old gravestones; one of a Frenchman from Dunkerque. I suppose he died prisoner in the military prison hard by; and one, the most pathetic memorial I ever saw, a poor school-slate in a wooden frame, with the inscription cut into it evidently by the father's own hand". This memorial is on the left just inside the gate; the inscription is: "Sacred to the memory of Catherine Ogg, the beloved child of James Henderson, 42nd Highlanders, who died at Greenlaw, on the 25th October 1869, aged 7 months". The other is in the north-east corner, and reads: "Ici repose Charles Cotier de Dunkerque, mort le 8 Janvier 1807". Part of the scenery here is worked into Chapter VI of *Weir of Hermiston*, and it haunted Stevenson to the last. "I shall never", he wrote to Crockett, "take that walk by the Fishers' Tryst and Glencorse. I shall never see Auld Reekie. I shall never set my foot again on the heather . . . . Do you know where the road crosses the burn under Glencorse Church? Go there and say a prayer for me. See that it is a sunny day; I would like it to be Sunday; but that's not possible in the premises; and stand on the right bank just where the road goes down into the water, and shut your eyes; and if I don't appear to you!"

"Pentland Rising"

Stevenson's earliest published effort, at sixteen, was an account of the Pentland Rising. His mother arranged for its publication with Andrew Elliot, the publisher, at 17 Princes Street (from which shop *Blackwood's Magazine* began its career); it is entitled *The Pentland Rising: a Page of History, 1666*, and was anonymous. Edmund Gosse in the Pentland edition of Stevenson's *Works* tells us that it was founded on a novel which the boy had begun at the age of 15. His father did not think it worthy of continuation, but thought that the author might, in a more sober historical spirit, preserve a record of the Rising. It is dated 28th November 1866. One hundred copies were printed of this seventy-two page pamphlet, in bright green cover, at a total cost of about three pounds fifteen shillings. Yet the publisher had afterwards to pay some twelve pounds for one of his own pamphlets when Stevenson became famous. The same feeling for the heather and Covenanting graves breathes in his fine lyric, "Blows the wind to-day", which is reminiscent of Pentland rambles.

Rullion Green Martyrs' Monument

At Flotterstone, between Glencorse Burn and the road, is the field where an annual service is held in summer, in commemoration of the battle of Rullion Green, which was fought on the eastern slope of Turnhouse Hill.

A monument on the edge of a wood above the cottage at Rullion Green bears the following inscriptions:—"Here and near to this place lyes the Reverend Mr. John Crookshanks and Mr. Andrew M'Cormack ministers of the Gospel and about fifty other true covenanting Presbyterians who were killed in this place in their own inecent self-defence and defence of the covenanting work of Reformation by Thomas Dalziel of Bins upon the 28 of November 1666 Rev. 12-11. Erected Sept. 28, 1738".

On the other side are the following verses:—

A cloud of witnesses lyes here,
Who for Christ's interest did appear,
For to restore true Liberty
Overturned then by Tyranny
And by Proud Prelats who did rage
Against the Lord's own heritage.

They sacrificed were for the Laws
Of Christ their King, his noble cause.
These heroes fought with great renown,
By falling got the Martyrs Crown.

A plaque on the railing around the monument reads: "This plaque, placed here in 1966 at the time of the third centenary of the battle, testifies to the enduring honour accorded to those Covenanters from Galloway and the West who rose in defence of civil and religious liberty. They marched on Edinburgh under the command of Colonel James Wallace, but the time was not ripe, and the country failed to support them.

On their retreat from the Capital they were overtaken by the Government forces and made their stand on this slope in the late afternoon. About 900 strong, and poorly equipped, they faced a trained army of over 3000. After heroic resistance they broke and fled into the winter night".

An entry in Penicuik Parish Records states that 3s. 4d. was paid shortly after the battle to the "bellman" for making "westlandmen's graves".

The Rising of 1666

The rising, which ended in the battle of Rullion Green, had its beginning in a scuffle at Dalry, in Galloway, with the soldiery. Sir James Turner had been commissioned by the Government to arrest all who signed the Covenant in the south-west of Scotland. The Covenanters in that quarter, driven from hearth and home, took action in defence; went to Dumfries; surprised Turner, taking him prisoner on the 4th November 1666; marched northwards to Ayr, where they received as recruit James Wallace, who had been in the Parliamentary Army in the English Civil Wars with the rank of colonel. A bailie of Dumfries reported this personally to the Privy Council, who instructed Dalziel of Binns to go westwards to Glasgow, and follow the Covenanters. Hearing of this they went eastwards to Lanark, numbering, at that time, about 1000 men, and then on to Bathgate. Their motive for marching in wretchedly wet and stormy weather, in this direction, was the information that reinforcements would be added to them at West Calder and Shotts. Reaching Bathgate, they turned towards Edinburgh on the assurance that there they would find friends in their favour, and arrived at Newbridge, near Kirkliston, on the 27th November, going thence to Colinton, where they remained till the morning of the eventful 28th. By this time the forces had fallen to 800 or 900, only partly under arms. Disappointed at not receiving any encouragement from Edinburgh, they resolved to return south to Clyde and Teviotdale, but Dalziel, who had followed them from Lanark to Currie, barred their return through the Pentlands. They therefore, on leaving Colinton, crossed the Braid Burn, passed Dreghorn Castle and Swanston, and, on reaching the Biggar Road, went south in the direction of West Linton. Crossing the Glencorse Burn at Flotterstone, or Ingliston as it was then called, they halted at Rullion Green.

Meanwhile, learning of their movements, Dalziel left Currie and marched through the Maiden's Cleuch (formerly called Cleuchmaidstone) (see Route 7) and past St. Catherine's Hope, with the view of intercepting them. When his troops came in sight, about noon, the Covenanters left the encampment at Rullion Green, and drew themselves up on the east side of Turnhouse Hill.

Here, to the south-west of where is now the Martyrs' Monument, the battle was fought under the leadership of Wallace, his infantry being in the centre, flanked on the left by the horse under Learmonth, and on the right by the horse under Barscobe. The Covenanters numbered 900 horse and foot. Dalziel's forces were variously estimated from 600 horse and 2000 foot, to 3000 foot besides horse.

On the first attack Dalziel was routed. The fight was resumed about sunset, and ended in the defeat and flight of the Covenanters. Turner, who had been with them as prisoner all the time, being now at liberty, rejoined his own party. About 150 were taken prisoners, the rest fled, many of them in the direction of Carlops. Local tradition affirms that some were killed by the Penicuik inhabitants, in the neighbourhood of Coates Farm, a place on the east side of the Biggar Road, and south of the battlefield. Others going westwards were lost in the Pentland bogs, bodies being discovered long after in perfect preservation. General Wallace escaped to Holland, and died there in 1676. The story of a Covenanter's grave near West Linton is given on a later page.

House o' Muir — Mauricewood

From House o' Muir farm, below Rullion Green, a road leads to Penicuik and a branch to Glencorse. In 1612 the city of Edinburgh was granted right of holding markets at House o' Muir; this was a great sheep market up to 1872.

Mauricewood, on the west side of the road to Penicuik, is where the terrible Mauricewood pit disaster occurred (1889). The pit had caught fire while seventy men and boys were underground.

Penicuik and the Paper Industry

To the south-west of Glencorse lies Penicuik, the centre of much that is interesting. Scott in boyhood met the original of "Monkbarns" of the *Antiquary* at Penicuik House. S. R. Crockett once occupied Bank House; and Professor Cossar Ewart once conducted his experiments with hybrids on this estate. Papermaking was for two centuries a considerable industry in Penicuik. The Valleyfield Mills of Messrs. Cowan had their start in 1708 by Mrs. Campbell, widow of Andrew Anderson, who had been Government printer. In 1773 the mills were acquired by Thomas Boswell, who sold them after six years' occupancy to Charles Cowan, merchant, Leith, who, with his two sons, Duncan and Alexander, carried on a moderately successful business with thirty workpeople, turning out two or three tons weekly of hand-made paper. In 1804 the firm bought Penicuik corn-mill, turned it into a paper-mill, and there for some time made paper for bank-notes. In 1811 the Valleyfield Mills were sold to the Government as a depot for French prisoners, about six thousand being confined there. A stone memorial has the inscription in English and French: "The mortal remains of 309 prisoners of war who died in this neighbourhood between 21st March 1811 and 26th July 1814 are interred near this spot". The mills were re-purchased by Mr. Cowan in 1818 and by continued extensions where required, and the introduction of the best and latest machinery, the firm took front rank in the trade. In 1965 the business was acquired by a company based in England; the mills were gradually closed down and paper making finally ceased in 1975.

Penicuik Worthies

In Penicuik neighbourhood, Mauricewood House was the residence of Dr. Joseph Bell, the prototype of "Sherlock Holmes". *The Memoirs of the Life of Sir John Clerk of Penicuik, Baron of Exchequer*, have been printed by the Scottish History Society. The founder of the family began life as a Montrose merchant, but made his fortune in Paris, acquired the lands of Penicuik and Wrightshouses, Edinburgh, and died in 1674.

Alexander Keith Johnston, the eminent map maker, and his brother, Sir William, who became Lord Provost of Edinburgh, were born at Kirkhill, now part of Penicuik. Henry Mackenzie lived for several summers at Auchendinny, as did also Mrs. Fletcher. "Christopher North" (Professor Wilson) came to Roslin for a time on the death of his wife.

In the churchyard, behind St. Mungo's Parish Church, are the remains of the old church of St. Kentigern, part of which has been incorporated in the burial enclosure of the Clerks of Penicuik. A plaque on the wall reads: "Rab & His Friends. Sacred to the memory of 'The Howgate Carrier' and his wife 'Ailie', who lie buried in this churchyard". They lived at Loanstone on the far side of the Esk.

3. Route 3—Craiglockhart or Slateford to Colinton 2 Miles

Craiglockhart — Redford — Colinton Castle — Mrs. Oliphant's "Open Door"—Notable Colinton Residents—Craiglockhart Dell—Boag's Mill—Paper Making—Colinton Dell—Redhall—Cromwell—Colinton Church—R. L. Stevenson and Rev. Dr. Balfour—Water of Leith "Walkway"—Spylaw House.

COLINTON, 4½ miles from the G.P.O., is a good centre for various Pentland Walks. From Craiglockhart or Slateford there is a choice of four routes to Colinton; (a) by Colinton Road, (b) by Craiglockhart Dell and Colinton Dell, (c) by Craiglockhart Drive and Colinton Dell, (d) by the public walk along the old railway line from Slateford.

(a) *By Colinton Road*

We can start at Craiglockhart Avenue or walk out from Morningside Road along Colinton Road, passing on the right Napier College, which incorporates the ancient tower of Merchiston Castle, where John Napier, the inventor of logarithms, was born in 1550. We next pass, on the left, George Watson's College, which was opened here in 1932 to replace the former college in Archibald Place, demolished to make room for an extension of the Royal Infirmary.

In Glenlockhart Road, between the two Craiglockhart Hills, Easter and Wester, is a narrow square tower believed to have been erected in the 15th century. The arched basement storey and the shattered walls of the second storey still remain but every vestige of the surrounding buildings has disappeared. There is evidence that Sir Simon Lockhart, from whose family the estate takes its name, purchased it from William Lamberton, its previous possessor, about the middle of the 13th century. The estate passed out of the hands of the Lockhart family and was for a time owned by Foulis of Colinton, an ancient family in the parish, and at one time the largest landowners. In 1630 Sir George Lockhart of Carnwath, bought back the property into his family, but in later centuries it passed through several owners; latterly into the hands of the Craiglockhart Estate Company which erected the Hydropathic, subsequently purchased by the Catholic Church for use as a convent and training college (now Craiglockhart College of Education).

REDFORD

Beyond the College and the reservoir of Lothian Region Water Department the road makes a turn to the right; looking over the large Redford Barracks, built in 1908-14 by the War Office on

Redford Estate, we see part of the Pentland range beginning at Caerketton and extending westwards by Allermuir, Capelaw, and on to White Hill above Bonaly. At Redford House, on the south of the Barracks, John Allen, who afterwards achieved fame as a writer and lecturer on physiology and on political and historical subjects, was born in 1770. He became physician to Lord Holland and his family in 1802, living at Holland House till his death in 1843. He was appointed Master of Dulwich College in 1818. Steeped in the history and traditions of the Whig politicians of the 18th century he was a valued contributor to the Edinburgh Review. Lord Macaulay designated him "a man of vast information and great conversational power"; while Lord Byron thought him "the best informed and one of the ablest men he knew." His great book was an *Enquiry into the Rise and Growth of the Royal Prerogative*, while he also published *A Vindication of the Ancient Independence of Scotland*.

Colinton Castle

Opposite Redford Barracks is Merchiston Castle School (which moved here from Merchiston Castle). In its grounds are the remains of the Colinton Castle, built in the 16th century, when the lands of Colinton were owned by James Foulis, an eminent Scottish lawyer, who became a judge in the new Court of Session instituted in 1532. His grandson married Agnes Heriot of Lymphoy, remembered by a tablet in Colinton Parish Church. In 1634 Alexander Foulis of Colinton was created a baronet of Nova Scotia. The second baronet, Sir James, suffered great losses from Cromwell's troops in 1650 (see below under Redhall), when they occupied Colinton Castle, and pillaged and burned both it and farms on the estate. Sir James was appointed a judge in 1661 with the title of Lord Colinton; in 1674 his son James was also appointed a judge, with the title of Lord Redford, and so father and son sat on the Bench at the same time until the father's death in 1688. In 1825 the baronetcy passed to a nephew, James Foulis of Woodhall; the present baronet has no residence in Scotland.

A small part of Colinton Estate, including the Castle, was bought towards the end of the 18th century by Sir William Forbes of Pitsligo, the eminent Edinburgh banker, who built there Colinton House, now part of Merchiston Castle School. His son, William, later the seventh baronet, and also a banker, was a college friend of Sir Walter Scott, and the successful rival for the hand of Miss Williamina Belches, Scott's early love. This did not affect the friendship and in the dark days of Scott's financial difficulties he recorded the help given by Sir William, acting "with the generosity of ancient faith and early friendship", in the arrangements with Scott's creditors. The third son of the marriage, James David Forbes, born in 1809, was elected Professor of Natural Philosophy in the University of Edinburgh at the age of 24, and was in later life Principal of the United College in the University of St. Andrews. He was one of the early climbers in the Alps, becoming an authority on the movement of glaciers, and wrote several books on his mountaineering experiences. The Forbes connection with Colinton House ended in 1830; the present baronet lives in New Zealand.

The house was later occupied by the first Lord Dunfermline, who, as James Abercromby (son of General Sir Ralph Abercromby), had been M.P. for Edinburgh, becoming Speaker of the House of Commons from 1835 to 1839, and given a peerage on demitting that office. A frequent visitor in his time was Dr. John Brown, author of *Rab and His Friends*. Lord Dunfermline, while gruff in manner, was full of courage, sincerity, and practical sagacity. He gave a letter to Lady Dunfermline one day in which he said, "Dr. Brown has told me I may die suddenly and therefore there may be no time for parting words, and besides, this would be painful for us both"; and then went on to say "You have been my comfort and my strength all my life".

Mrs. Oliphant's "Open Door"

Mrs. Oliphant found a setting here for one of her *Stories of the Seen and Unseen*, called *The Open Door*. Here is her description of the house: "Brentwood (Colinton House) stands on that fine and wealthy slope of country, one of the richest in Scotland, which lies between the Pentland Hills and the Firth. In clear weather you could see the blue gleam like a bent bow, embracing the wealthy fields and scattered houses of the great estuary on one side of you and on the other the blue heights, not gigantic like those we have been used to, but just high enough for all the glories of the atmosphere, the play of clouds and sweet reflections, which gives to a hilly country an interest and a charm which nothing else can emulate."

The village of "Brentwood"—or Colinton—comes in for a slight descriptive sketch, lying almost under the house, on the other side of the deep little ravine, down which ran a stream which ought to have been lovely and frolicsome, but which had been sacrificed to trade and was grimy with paper-making. That side of the dell was clothed with fine trees; the village lay in the hollow and climbed, with prosaic houses, the other side. The glen or dell was beautiful at all seasons, and the writer did not dislike the interior of the old-fashioned pewed and galleried church which has been rebuilt. In the park which surrounded the house were the ruins of the former mansion of Brentwood, which the novelist makes, as it is in reality, much smaller and less important than the solid Georgian edifice which she inhabited. The old building had the remains of a tower, an indistinguishable mass of masonwork, overgrown with ivy. The ruins are further described with a doorway open and vacant, free to all the winds, to the rabbits and every wild creature. "A door that led to nothing—closed once—perhaps, with anxious care, bolted and guarded, now void of any meaning. It impressed me, I remember, from the first". Round the ruin, a pretty domestic story, with its mystery, is cunningly woven: a story which is rationally explained at last, and which we need not spoil by trying to repeat for those who have once read it or may still have the pleasure of doing so.

James Ballintine, the Scottish author (1808-77), describes Colinton in his *Miller of Deanhaugh*, with "its romantic valley, its line of cottages embedded in the hollows; its kail yairds, and their rows of currant bushes; its sylvan pathways threaded the masses of wood, deep, deep down in the beautiful Dell."

Notable Colinton Residents

While resident at Colinton Bank, Dr. Thomas Murray published his interesting *Biographical Annals of the Parish of Colinton* in 1863. Dr. Murray, before his death at Lasswade in 1872, had been a pioneer in many important departments of life, and in the successful printing firm later known as Morrison & Gibb. He was a friend and correspondent of Thomas Carlyle and Alexander Murray. He wrote lives of Samuel Rutherford, Leighton and Wycliffe, and was one of the founders of the Philosophical Institution in 1846. For thirty years he was Secretary of the Edinburgh School of Art. Dr. Pryde calls him the autocrat of that school in its formative period—the presiding genius of the place. He had unfailing tact and never made an enemy. He had written for Sir David Brewster's *Edinburgh Encyclopaedia*, as his friend Carlyle had also done.

Other notable residents have been Henry Mackenzie, commemorated by a tablet on the cottage at the top of Bridge Street, "In this house lived Henry Mackenzie, author of *The Man of Feeling*. Born 25th August 1745. Died 14th January 1831"; and Dr. Alison, Professor of the Theory and Practice of Physic in the Edinburgh University, son of the Rev. Mr. Alison, who died at Woodville, author of the *Essay on the Nature and Principles of Taste*, and father of Sir Archibald Alison, the author of the *History of Europe* from the French Revolution. The Rev. Dr. Lewis Balfour, James Gillespie, and others, are mentioned in later pages.

(b) *By Craiglockhart Dell and Colinton Dell*

The path through Craiglockhart Dell begins at Slateford, where the Lanark Road crosses the Water of Leith. The "Slate Ford", where the stream escaped from its steep banks, was an important crossing; here Prince Charles and his army met the Magistrates of Edinburgh in September 1745 to discuss the surrender of the city, and at Grays Mill, a little downstream, the Prince rested overnight before his entry into Edinburgh.

Shortly the path passes an old stone grotto constructed beside a small ravine; beyond it a steep path goes up to the dovecot with the Otterburn coat of arms (see below under Redhall).

Boag's Mill

Another quarter mile up the dell, where the stream is crossed by a stout stone bridge, at one time the entrance to Redhall, is the level haugh where stood Boag's Mill; what little remains of the old mill has been incorporated in the stonework attached to a modern dwelling house. Other evidence of the mill is seen in the short stretch surviving of the mill lade. Boag's Mill is the name on old maps; now it is Bogs Mill. It was at one time a waulkmill (where cloth is cleaned and thickened) and later a corn mill, and was converted to paper making in 1717. Here was made some of the banknote paper used for Scottish banknotes in the 18th century; while it was being made bank officials came and lived at the mill house to ensure complete control of the special paper. Later it was a snuff mill and latterly in use as a grain mill until destroyed by fire in 1924.

Paper-making

Paper making has been a considerable industry on the Water of Leith for four centuries, starting in 1590 with the first paper mill in Scotland at Dalry. The earliest paper mill above Slateford was started in 1681 at Upper Spylaw above Colinton; the next, in operation in 1714, had the curious name of Jinkabout, of which not a stone remains. It stood where the gardens are now, on the north bank of the Water of Leith about half way between Slateford and Bogs Mill. Dr. A. G. Thomson in his book on *The Paper Industry in Scotland* tells us that in the 18th century the Water of Leith paper mills were producing at times from 20 to 30 percent of Scotland's paper, from some nine or ten mills. All this paper was hand made. The water power was also used for other mills; the writer of the *Statistical Account* for Colinton Parish says that in 1794 the Water of Leith in the course of ten miles drove 71 mills, including 4 paper mills, 5 snuff mills, and 20 flour mills.

From Bogs Mill the better path up the dell is on the north bank, recrossing the stream just short of Kate's Mill, of which the mill house survives, with alterations, as a dwelling house. This mill was a waulk mill, converted to paper making in 1783 by John Balfour, the owner of Boag's Mill, and named Kate's Mill after his wife. Balfour had experienced some difficulties in providing adequate accommodation for the bank officials at Boag's Mill, and at Kate's Mill the arrangements included ample cellars for their wine. This mill was large enough for a paper making machine to be installed by 1832; it was burnt down in 1890 and not rebuilt. Immediately beyond Kate's Mill is Redhall Mill, where paper making began in 1717 and continued until 1750; it was later a grain mill and now makes wood-flour for plastics.

Colinton Dell

Continuing up Colinton Dell the path reaches the village at Colinton Manse. Robert Louis Stevenson in *Memories and Portraits*, has this to say about the Water of Leith and its mills:

"I have named, among many rivers that make music in my memory, that dirty Water of Leith. Often and often I desire to look upon it again, and the choice of a point of view is easy to me. It should be at a certain water-door, embowered in shrubbery. The river is there dammed back for the service of the flour mill just below, so that it lies deep and darkling, and the sand slopes into brown obscurity with a glint of gold; and it has but newly been recruited by the borrowings of the snuff mill just above, and these, tumbling merrily in, shake the pool to its black heart, fill it with drowsy eddies, and set the curded froth of many other mills solemnly steering to and fro upon the surface. Or so it was when I was young; for change, and the masons, and the pruning knife have been busy; and if I could hope to repeat a cherished experience, it must be on many and impossible conditions.

It was a place in that time like no other; the garden cut into provinces by a great hedge of beech, and overlooked by the church and the terrace of the churchyard . . . the smell of water rising from all around, with an added tang of paper-mills; the sound of water everywhere, and the sound of mills—the wheel and the dam singing their alternate strain; the birds on every bush and from every corner of the overhanging woods pealing out their notes until the air throbbed with them; and in the midst of this the manse." The mills that once stood near the manse have since been demolished.

(c) *By Craiglockhart Drive*

Redhall

Colinton Dell can also be reached from the College of Education in Colinton Road by going down Craiglockhart Avenue to the church and turning left there along Craiglockhart Drive. Beyond the houses on the north side of the Drive is Redhall, whose history goes back to the 14th century, when it belonged to Sir Alexander Menzies who succeeded to the Menzies estates in Perthshire. The original barony of Redhall included the whole area south-east of the Water of Leith up to the Pentland Hills, including Colinton, Dreghorn and Swanston. Sir William Cunningham held the barony in the 15th century; then in the early 16th century, when Colinton Castle was sold to Sir James Foulis, Redhall was sold about the same time to Sir Adam Otterburn of Auldhame, who, like Foulis, became a member of the new Court of Session in 1532. A 16th century panel with the Otterburn arms—an otter's head, a crest, and two wyverns for supporters, and the motto "De virtute in virtutem"—taken from the old house, is built into the north side of the splendid 18th century hexagonal dovecot standing on the edge of the dell behind Graysmill School. It can be seen by going down the burn on the east side of the school. Sir Adam also served for two terms as Provost of Edinburgh and represented the city in the Scots Parliament. The estate passed to Sir James Hamilton of Hoprig in 1614 when he married Anne Otterburn. The events of 1650 (described below) impoverished the Hamiltons and they sold Redhall in 1662. In 1672 the owner was the notorious John Chiesley of Dalry who in 1689 shot Sir George Lockhart, the President of the Court of Session, because of a Court decision in family litigation. After other changes in ownership the estate was acquired in 1755 by George Inglis, who built the present house, with outbuildings made partly from the stones from the ruins of the old castle. George Inglis was succeeded by his nephew, Captain John Inglis, R.N. who commanded *H.M.S. Belliquex*, at the battle of Camperdown. He received the freedom of the City of Edinburgh and was promoted Vice-Admiral in 1805. The house is now a children's home.

Cromwell and Redhall

In July 1650 Cromwell entered Scotland with his army by the order of the English Commonwealth, and on August 13th took up his position on the Braid Hills. He planned to take possession of Queensferry, where his ships could land supplies, and to do this had to pass between Corstorphine Hill and Edinburgh. Meantime, the Scottish army, under David Leslie, had taken up a position on the south side of Edinburgh facing the English army. Cromwell began his plan by moving his troops to Colinton, and Leslie moved his army to Corstorphine Hill. Redhall stood in Cromwell's way and its siege is described in the *Diary* kept by John Nicoll, an Edinburgh lawyer: "Generall Cromwell and his airmy haifing past throw this kingdome fra Berwik to the place of Colingtoun, without ony oppositoun maid be ony of the gentillmenis houssis by the way quhair they past, until they come to the hous of Reidhall, within thrie myles be west Edinburgh; in the quhilk hous of Reidhall, the Laird of Reidhall with thriescoir sodgeris lay, with provisioun, and keipit and defendit the hous aganes the Englisches, and gallit his sodgeris, and pat thame bak severall tymes with the los of sindry sodgeris. The Englisches Generall, taking this very grevouslie, that such a waik hous sould hald out aganes him, and be ane impediment in his way, he and his airmy lying so neir unto it; thairfoir he causit draw his cannoun to the hous, and thair, fra four houris in the morning till ten in the foirnune that day, he causit the cannoun to play on this hous, encampit a great number of his sodgeris about it, with pik and musket, but all to lytill purpos; for the Laird and the pepill in the hous defendit valiantlie evir till thair powder failled; and eftir it failled they did not give over, ever luiking for help fra owr awin airmy, quha wes then lying at Corstorphyn, within thrie quarteris of ane myle to the hous; of quhais help thai was disapoynted. Generall Cromwell perceaving thair powder to be gone, and that no assistance wes gevin thame, he causit pittardis to be brocht to the hous, quhairwith he blew up the dures; enterit the hous at dures and windois, and eftir slaughter on both sydes, (bot much moir to the Englisches then the Scottish) tuik all that wer in the hous prissoneris, tirred them naked, seased on all the money and guidis that wer thairin, quhilk wes much, be ressoun that sindry gentillmen about haid put thair guidis thair for saiftie. So this hous and pepill thairin wer taken in the sicht and face of our airmy . . . Eftir the enymie haid takin the Laird of Reidhall prissoner, he theireftir put him at liberty commending much his valour and activitie for holding out so stoutlie aganes him that hous of Reidhall." ("tirred"—stripped).

Colinton Church

The Colinton Dell path ends at Colinton Church. The ancient church of the parish dedicated to St. Cuthbert and founded about the year 1095 was at Hailes and is supposed to have stood on the site of Hailes House which stands on the plateau, a quarter mile to the north, above Colinton Dell. Hailes House (now a hotel) dates from the end of the 18th century; it was at one time inhabited by Samuel Anderson, banker, who left a small endowment to the poor of Colinton. To the north of it once stood Easter Hailes, residence of George Drummond, six times Lord Provost of Edinburgh, who founded the Royal Infirmary. Hailes Quarry (now filled in) yielded a fortune to its proprietor when the building boom was in progress in Edinburgh in the early 19th century.

The original church at Hailes was gifted at the beginning of the 12th century by Ethelred, Earl of Fife, second son of Malcolm

Canmore, to Dunfermline Abbey; later it was transferred to Holyrood Abbey, later again to the Preceptory of St. Anthony at Leith. It is said that it was destroyed on the Earl of Hertford's invasion of 1544–45; if so, it must have been restored, as a church at Easter Hailes is shown on a map of the Lothians dated c.1610. A tablet in the porch of the present church says that another church was placed here in the year 1636: it was rebuilt in 1771 and rebuilt again in 1908.

During the time of the first church, strict discipline was exercised on the Sabbath-breaker and the intemperate, who had to submit to public rebuke and even to the embrace of the "jougs" and clothing in sackcloth. The absence of fixed pews must have been very disconcerting, each hearer bringing his or her own stool. Thus we read that in 1744: "Isabel Colquhoun being summoned to this dyet, and compearing, was charged with disturbing the neighbours about her in time of sermon. To which the said Isabel answered that she, being the oldest possessor of a chair in the body of the kirk, she thought that the neighbours in Bonally should have more respect to her than toss her chair up and down the kirk as they often did, and that all the noise she made was to get her chair where it had stood three score of years, but that she was sorry for any offence she had given"—whereupon she was "rebuikit" by the kirk session.

R. L. Stevenson and the Rev. Dr. Balfour

The Rev. Lewis Balfour, D.D., minister here from 1823 to 1860, is the centre of much of its interest, partly on his own account and also for the sake of his grandson, Robert Louis Stevenson, who, because of ill health, frequently came to stay with his maternal grandfather in Colinton Manse until Dr. Balfour's death in 1860.

In *Memories and Portraits*, Stevenson has given a picture of his venerable grandfather: "I read him, as a man of singular simplicity of nature; unemotional, and hating the display of what he felt; a lover of his life and innocent habits to the end. We children admired him; partly for his beautiful face and silver hair, for none more than children are concerned for beauty and, above all, for beauty in the old; partly for the solemn light in which we observed him once a week, the observed of all observers in the pulpit." Into the room where the old man sat in the midst of a library of "bloodless books", the little boy was sent by his mother to repeat a psalm. It was that lyric which no Scotsman hears sung away from home without a moisture in his eyes and a lump in his throat—"I to the hills will lift mine eyes." This is how the man records the childish experience:—

"I went in quaking with fear . . .

Thy foot He'll not let slide, nor will
He slumber that thee keeps,

it ran—a strange conglomerate of the unpronounceable, a sad model to set in childhood before one who was himself to be a versifier, and a task in recitation which merited reward. And I must suppose the old man thought so too, for he took me in his arms and kissed me, and gave me a little kindly sermon for my psalm; so that for that day we were clerk and parson."

In the churchyard a massive coffin-shaped iron case lies near the gate, a relic of "resurrectionist" days. Behind the church are memorials to the old families of the parish who were buried here. One reads "Within rest the remains of James Gillespie of Spylaw . . . died 8 April 1797 . . . who bequeathed the bulk of his fortune for the endowment of an hospital in the City of Edinburgh for the maintenance of aged men and women and for a free school for the education of poor boys." Next is the memorial to the Rev. Lewis Balfour, D.D. 1777–1860; born at Pilrig, for 37 years minister at Colinton. One memorial is to David Pitcairn of Dreghorn, who died in 1709, after having five sons and seven daughters, whose descendants included many who became eminent in their professions. Another memorial is to a later owner of Dreghorn, R. A. Macfie, who died in 1893. The oldest memorial is a tablet inside the church: "Heir lyis ane honorabil woman A Hiriot spous to J. Foulis of Colling Toun was quha died 8 August 1593." A sundial on the corner of the church on the left of the porch has the date of 1630 and the name Sir James Foulles. The family of Foulis owned the lands of Colinton at least from 1531. The bridge over the Water of Leith dates from 1686.

(d) *By the Old Railway "Walkway": Slateford to Colinton*

The old railway line which now provides the pleasant walk from Slateford to Colinton and Balerno was opened to passenger traffic on 1st August 1874. Reporting the event the *Edinburgh Courant* of 3rd August said: "On Saturday the Colinton, Juniper Green, Currie and Balerno branch of the Caledonian Railway was opened for passenger traffic and was taken advantage of by large numbers . . . As it is made to follow the windings of the glen, and for the most part keeps close to the stream, its course is a continuous series of sharp curves. This, while in no way interfering with the comfort of the passengers, enables lovers of the picturesque scenery to view with ease the numerous lovely little "bits" for which Colinton Glen is famous, and which hitherto, generally speaking, have been available only to good pedestrians . . . On Saturday it was amusing to see the terror and perturbation of the horses, cows, and domestic poultry at the sight of so unusual a visitant as a railway train". Before the competition of road transport the trains ran hourly, with the last train back to town from Balerno at 10 p.m.

The line was closed on 30th October, 1943, and the track is now a footpath, the Water of Leith Walkway, providing an easy gradient in its rise of some 300 feet up the valley of the Water of Leith. The shortest access to the path is by Redhall Bank Road, which branches left from the Lanark Road a quarter mile beyond Slateford; the same point can be reached by walking up Craiglockhart Dell from Slateford and at the stone bridge crossing the Water of Leith to Bogsmill Road, which goes uphill and under the old railway bridge.

Spylaw House

The path runs along the north slope of Colinton Dell for half a mile. Then comes a curving tunnel (with lights), 160 yards long, cut through the rock bordering Colinton Dell, to the former Colinton Station. Spylaw Park and Spylaw House (now a Scout hostel) are next seen on the left. The house has part dating from the 17th century; in the second half of the 18th century it was enlarged by James Gillespie who carried on a snuff mill beneath the house, in the old part at the rear, for nearly forty years until his death in 1797, in the process amassing a fortune which he left for the erection in Edinburgh of a hospital for the aged. Built in 1805, Gillespie's Hospital is now used as workshops by the Royal Blind Asylum. His old shop is still to be seen, with a medallion portrait of him upon it, on the north side of the High Street of Edinburgh. The story is told that when he acquired a carriage and was looking for a motto to be placed on it Henry Erskine facetiously suggested:

Wha wad hae thocht it
That noses had bocht it?

Beyond Spylaw Park is the tall building occupied as offices and laboratories of the Forth River Purification Board and the complex of buildings at West Mills, site of another paper mill established c.1825. For the continuation of this walk see Route 4b.

4. Route 4—Colinton to Juniper Green and Balerno

4 to 6 Miles

Juniper Green—Dr. John Brown's Gallop—Baberton—Currie or Kinleith—Currie Bridge—Famous Residents in Currie Parish—The "Walkway"—Woodhall Mills—Lennox Tower—Balerno—Woodhall—Malleny—Torduff and Clubbiedean Reservoirs—Kinleith—Poet's Glen.

BETWEEN Colinton and Currie there are no less than five routes, (a) by Juniper Green, (b) by the old railway path, (c) by Woodhall and Blinkbonny, (d) by Torphin, and (e) by Torduff and Clubbiedean Reservoirs. Four of these routes continue to Balerno.

(a) *By Juniper Green*

There may be times when a bracing walk along the road can be enjoyed, and this road from Colinton to Balerno has the merit of providing attractive views across the Water of Leith valley to the foothills of the Pentlands. The road through Colinton is carried high above the Water of Leith and the old railway line, by a modern bridge; before its day one went down what is now Spylaw Street and crossed by the old bridge (built in 1686) and then made a steep ascent past the church to reach the Lanark Road. At the cross roads beyond Colinton a left hand turn brings us to Juniper Green, a modern village first mentioned in records in 1707. Thomas Carlyle lived here for a short time after his marriage, and had his first experience in the difficulties of housekeeping.

Dr. John Brown has related a gallop with his father to Juniper Green. "My father had not been on a horse for nearly twenty years. He mounted, and rode off. He soon got teased with the short, pattering steps of Goliath, and looked wistfully up at me, and longingly to the tall chestnut, stepping once for Goliath's twice, like the Don striding beside Sancho. So we changed. I remember how noble he looked; how at home; his white hair and his dark eyes, his erect, easy, accustomed seat. He soon let his eager horse slip gently away. It was first *evasit*, he was off, Goliath and I jogging on behind; then *erupit*, and in a twinkling *evanuit*. I saw them last flashing through the arch under the Canal, his white hair flying. I was uneasy, though from his riding I knew he was as yet in command, so I put Goliath to his best, and having passed through Slateford, I asked a stonebreaker if he saw a gentleman on a chestnut horse. 'Has he white hair?' 'Yes'. 'And een like a gled's?' 'Yes'. 'Weel then, he's fleein' up the road like the wund; he'll be at Little Vantage' (about nine miles off) 'in nae time if he haud on'. I never once sighted him, but on coming into Juniper Green, there was his steaming chestnut at the gate, neighing cheerily to Goliath".

On the right, about half a mile away, is Baberton House, built by John Murray, the King's Master of Works, in 1622/23, in the style of Heriot's Hospital. The ex-King of France, Charles X, came to Baberton, for shooting quarters, while residing at Holyrood. The date 1622 appears over one of the windows of Baberton House. The lands can be traced back to the 14th century, proprietors' names having been Cissor, Crawford, Forrester, Wardlaw, Elphinstone, and Sir James Murray, Master of Works to King James. In the circled pediment of one of the windows are the initials, I.M. and K.W. (James Murray and Katherine Weir, his wife, 1622). About the time of the Reformation there was a Presbyterian meeting-house at Baberton.

Currie

Currie Church is a foundation of mediaeval times, dedicated to St. Kentigern or St. Mungo, in 1296. In 1627 Currie was a special rectory and parsonage of the Archdeacon of Lothian, from whom it was taken and bestowed by King James VI on the city of Edinburgh. There is a monument in the churchyard to Adam and Matthew Lichton, the first two Protestant ministers of Currie (1568-1631). The present church was built in 1785. The ruined choir of the old parish church, on the east side of the present church, has been restored to form a session house as a memorial to the Rev. David C. Stewart, minister of Currie from 1898 to 1950. Within are several mural tombstones: a Templar's tombstone, dating from the 13th century, and the Invergowrie memorial dated 1670. An ingenious sun-dial, the work of Robert Palmer, schoolmaster, standing in front of the church, is also worthy of attention. Palmer planned the old school, the building on the right as you face the church. Along with Sir William Gibson Craig, Palmer was originator of the Caledonian Curling Club, and started Currie Curling Club. The Currie communion cups bear the marks of David Heriot, who followed George Heriot as Deacon of the Craft, in the last year of the 16th century. A round hollow piece of silver, having remains of gilding on it, part of the stalk of a crucifix, or altar candlestick, was unearthed here after 1784, but has disappeared.

Currie Bridge

At the north end of Currie Bridge are the scanty remains of the meal mill, the kiln, and the old inn, which it is said had a window at the east end, a handy place through which to dispense liquor. It is mentioned in James Grant's *Harry Ogilvie*. Anglers frequented the inn in the old days when kept by Marion Cunningham, about whom this rhyme has been preserved:—

At Currie brig end,
Auld Marion was kend,
For forty years at least,
By the great and the sma',
The raggit an' bra',
The dominie, elder, and priest.

The deep waters below Currie Bridge gave rise to the saying "As deep as Currie Brig", indicating shrewdness and selfish cunning.

At the roadside, beyond the bridge and opposite the smithy, is the "Corslet", a square chamfered pillar, 3 feet 4 inches in height, which formerly stood in a part of the south strip of Riccarton Estate known locally as the "Barlie Coort", i.e. the Burlaw Court, the place where local people met to discuss parish matters.

The grounds of the former mansion house of Riccarton, to the north of Currie, are now occupied by the campus of Heriot Watt University. The foundation stone was laid in 1971 of the first phase of the University buildings, which will eventually replace the building in Chambers Street in Edinburgh, better known as the Heriot Watt College before it acquired University status.

Famous Residents in Currie Parish

Famous residents in Currie Parish have been Sir John Skene (1543-1617) of Curriehill, who was one of those chosen to carry through the negotiations concerning the marriage of Princess Anne of Denmark with James VI. He was also one of the Commissioners to treat for a union between England and Scotland, and published important legal books. Sir Thomas Craig (1538-1608) of Riccarton, founder of the Craig family, was author of *Jus Feudale and De Unione*, printed by the Scottish History Society. Margaret, his eldest daughter, married Alexander Gibson, of Durie, and from this branch, the present representatives are descended. Another daughter married James Johnston of Warriston, merchant in Edinburgh, one of their children being Archibald Johnston, who was raised to the Bench as Lord Warriston. As a Presbyterian leader, he incurred the enmity of Charles II, and was executed in Edinburgh in 1663 and buried in Greyfriars Churchyard. Currie Memorial Hall was erected in memory of Robert Gibson-Craig of Riccarton, who was killed in the Boer War. A native of Currie in more recent times was Dougal Haston, one of the first two Britons, and the first Scot, to reach the summit of Mount Everest.

(b) *By the "Walkway"—the Old Railway Line*

The first part of this "walkway" from Slateford to Colinton, is described in Route 3. At Colinton we can join it either at Spylaw Park (entered from Spylaw Road or by the steps down from Bridge Road), or at West Mills, reached by going along Woodhall Road and down West Mills Road.

Beyond West Mills the valley narrows and where we cross to the north bank the weir and rocks provide quite a waterfall after rain. Soon we pass on our left a tall building, with its gable to the path, which has developed from the original Upper Spylaw Mill, the earliest paper mill above Slateford, started here in 1681 and operating for some 20 to 30 years. Its later history includes periods as a snuff mill, and as a dairy. On the far side of the stream are the buildings of Mossy Mill, at one time a waulk mill and converted to paper making in the 19th century. It was closed down in 1972.

Woodhall Mills

Next on the route is Woodhall Grain Mill, also known as Inglis's Mill, employed in milling and in drying grain, one of the early 18th century mills. Beyond it, where the path strikes the river again is a broken down weir and the foundations of the old mill lade. Round the next bend as you approach the newer part of the buildings of Woodhall Paper Mill, the storage sheds now occupying the site of Juniper Green Station, the path crosses the outflow from an old snuff mill, producing snuff until 1940, whose crumbling ruins can be seen on the right. Where the path and the road to the paper mill run together, keep to the right to pass the mill, which has been going under various owners since 1792. It is the only paper mill in the valley now manufacturing, except that instead of the "Superfine writing and printing paper" which it once produced its output now is paperboard for boxes.

Immediately past the paper mill the path crosses the Water of Leith. Just beyond the bridge can be seen a mill lade, all that remains of the snuff mill built in 1749 which made snuff here until 1920. Across the stream is East Mill House, with a garden laid out on the roof of the basement of the old grain mill, mentioned in the 17th century and in use until 1900. The remains of another mill lade are seen on the right after passing under a road bridge. Next we come to the large complex of buildings which, until production ceased in 1966, was Kinleith Paper Mill, established here in or about 1792, and when working, the largest mill on the Water of Leith, with over 300 employees at one time. Now it is named Kinleith Industrial Estate. The route is now crossed by a path which comes down the Kinleith Burn, the "Poet's Glen", described on another page. Between the mill dam and Currie Brig is a public garden with Mungo's Well; on the left are Currie Kirk and old school.

Currie

Where the old railway bridge crosses the Kirkgate you look down on Currie Brig, and on the ruined kiln of the old meal mill. After passing the site of Currie Station we see shortly on our right Currie Bowling Green, opened in 1875. On our left is a strong retaining wall built for the railway; this is referred to by Dougal Haston, who reached the summit of Everest in 1975, in his book *In High Places* as a place where he practised climbing in his youth with six inch nails for pitons and clothesline for rope. Then on the right are the buildings of Kinauld Leather Works, now employed in tanning pigskins, calfskins, and goatskins into light leather for binding and other purposes, after having served a variety of uses since built as a paper mill in 1788 by Nisbet and Macniven. According to the *Statistical Account* of Currie Parish the paper trade in 1792 employed children from 10 or 12 years of age, as well as adults and people too old to work out of doors. For some reason this mill was known as the Balerno Mill. Next on the left is Kinauld Farm, another place with a long history, which in the early part of the 19th century was a distillery.

Lennox Tower

On the high ground across the water may be seen between the trees the ivy clad ruin of Lennox Tower, dating from the 15th century, with walls 7½ feet thick. In its round headed entrance doorway is still seen the aperture for a sliding bar behind the door. It had a vaulted ground floor, and a waggon-vaulted great hall above. It is said to have been an occasional residence of Queen Mary, and a favourite hunting place of James VI when it was owned by the Lennox family in the 16th century. According to the writer of the *Statistical Account* in 1792 it had a subterranean passage to the river (so that no enemy could deprive the inhabitants of water), which had only been shut up a short time before the *Account* was written because cattle were apt to go down into it. It is said that once, during a siege, when the garrison was hard pressed for provisions, and the enemy was confident of starving them out, one of the besieged who had gone down this passage for water, accidentally caught some fish in his bucket, which the governor boastingly hung out in sight of the besiegers. On seeing this unexpected sight, the assailants raised the siege, deeming it a hopeless attempt to starve out a garrison so mysteriously supplied.

Balerno

Continuing along the path we cross a bridge over an old mill lade and pass the Old Mill House of Newmills, once a grain mill and mentioned in the early 17th century.

The path ends at the site of Balerno Station, where the road crosses the Water of Leith and then forks, one road going up to the older part of the village (a through route for pedestrians only), and the new road sweeping round to the left to go up past the village to the reservoirs and the hills. Balerno began with, and expanded on, paper making. It started in 1799 at Byrnie Mill, of which all that remains is a little stonework on the west bank of the Bavelaw Burn, just above the footbridge on the path from Malleny House; on a map of c.1610 the village name was spelt Byrney. Next came Balerno Bank Mill in 1805; this was rebuilt or expanded to form the present block of buildings on the left above the main street, and only in recent years has paper making been discontinued and the work restricted to the special coating of paper made elsewhere.

(c) *By Woodhall Road*

An alternative route from Colinton to Balerno goes along the south side of the Water of Leith valley, starting in Woodhall Road, which leaves Colinton Road at the top of the brae descending into Colinton village. In the wall after No. 38 is an old stone with the inscription "5 miles from the GPO Edinburgh. Erected to regulate the post horse duties payable by hackney coach 1824". Just beyond is West Mills Road leading down to the valley walk.

Woodhall House

Woodhall Road continues for another mile, and ends at the house of Woodhall, opposite Juniper Green. At one time the estate was owned by the family of Foulis, a branch of the family of Foulis of Colinton, who acquired the estate in the 17th century from the Cunninghams. Woodhall gave a title to Hugh Cunningham, an advocate who became a Lord of Session in 1637 and took his seat as Lord Woodhall. George Foulis, a son of James Foulis of Colinton and Agnes Heriot of Lymphoy, married Janet, the daughter of George Bannatyne, who, in the 16th century collected most of the Scottish poetry of the 15th and early 16th centuries, and compiled a folio of some 800 pages of the poems. This manuscript, the *Bannatyne Manuscript*, was preserved by the later Foulises at Woodhall and in 1770 presented to the Advocates' Library, now the National Library of Scotland; since that time two printed editions have been published. The Foulis connection with Woodhall ceased in 1932; it is now occupied by a Roman Catholic community. The grounds around the house are bypassed by a cart road on the left, starting at the farm, and continued by a footpath outside the grounds until it joins the road which comes over the Water of Leith to the houses at Blinkbonny. Beyond the hamlet is the Kinleith Burn, which comes down the "Poet's Glen". A footpath across the burn provides a short cut to Currie Kirk, whilst a path which leaves the road at the west side of Glenburn Hotel grounds goes up to Mount Parhassus where James Thomson lived (see below).

Either the road, or the short cut by the path, takes us to Currie Kirk and here, opposite the churchyard, is the road to Malleny House, a private road but open to pedestrians. In a quarter mile we come to a strip of trees known as Duncan's Belt, where will be seen on the right of the road a grave stone inscribed: "In this small enclosure are a number of stone coffins of various dimensions: they were discovered in December 1820 by the proprietor Lieut. General Thomas Scott . . . Renewed by District Council 1971". The road goes on, over an old stone bridge known as the "Deil's Brig" to Lymphoy House, which has in its grounds the ruins of Lennox Tower, described above.

Malleny

In another half mile we reach Malleny. This estate was owned in the 15th century by the family of Knightson and after several changes in ownership was acquired in the first half of the 17th century by Sir William Scott of Clerkington, a branch of the Scotts of Buccleuch. The present mansion was probably built by the Scotts in the 17th century, judging from the style of architecture and the Scott coat of arms above the front door. In 1882 the estate was bought by Lord Rosebery and more recently was owned by the late Commander Robert Gore-Browne Henderson, R.N., whose widow gave Malleny House and Garden to the National Trust for Scotland in 1968. The very attractive garden, but not the house, is open to the public from May to September; four yew trees are the remainder of twelve trees said to have been planted in 1603. Opposite the approach to the Garden an iron gate and an avenue of trees lead to the mausoleum of the Scotts (no admission). From the entrance to the car park a path leading to a footbridge over the Bavelaw Burn provides an alternative approach to Balerno village.

"These northern skirts of the Pentlands", says John Geddie in *The Water of Leith*, "are something of a backwater in the national annals. The stream of great national events, swinging strongly round the eastern end of the range towards the capital, has taken a more northern line to the west. But great men and noteworthy deeds have not been wholly wanting. One need not go back to 'Old unhappy times and battles long ago' when forgotten warriors built their camps and cairns on the Warklaw and Ravelrig Hills, or on the crest of the Kaimes. We know that kings feasted at Bavelaw, and winded the bugle-horn, and hunted hart and roe on Threipmuir; that moss-trooping Elliots and Armstrongs and Scotts have pricked thither on foray to lift the kye and gear of the Lothians' lairds and tenants, and escape back to Tweedside by the Borestane Pass, or the Cauldstane-slap . . . The Templars, and after them the Knights Hospitallers from Torphichen Preceptory, must have been not unfamiliar figures in the lands that belonged to them on the Water of Leith, now partly covered by Harperrig Loch".

(d) *By Torduff and Clubbiedean Reservoirs*

The fourth of the routes between Colinton and Balerno and a very picturesque one goes by the reservoirs, reached from Woodhall Road by going up Fernielaw Avenue, the third road on the left after passing West Mills Road. The first reservoir is Torduff, lying like a West Highland loch in a deep and narrow hollow behind Torphin Hill. Looking back from here we have a fine view over Bonaly Tower and Colinton, and over Edinburgh to Arthur's Seat in the background like a couchant lion. It was the view from Torphin Hill which H. W. Williams said most resembled that of Athens. At the far end of the reservoir the road crosses the burn beside a miniature waterfall, and climbs to the level of Clubbiedean Reservoir, with its picturesque background of trees. At the south west end of the trees are the remains of a prehistoric fort—two concentric earthen ramparts with a ditch between them and another on the outside, with a length of 164 feet internally and a maximum width of 124 feet. The ramparts are in parts still 5 feet high.

Kinleith — Poet's Glen

The road continues round the hill to East Kinleith Farm on the Kinleith Burn, here flowing down the deep "Poet's Glen", so named from James Thomson, the Weaver Poet, who lived at Mount Parnassus, in one of the cottages on the west bank of the glen. A stone, with an inscription headed "Jamie Tamson's Helicon", and a verse of poetry, is down at a spring and pool by the burn, but it is virtually inaccessible as the way down to it is much overgrown and partly blocked by fallen trees.

Kinleith was previously known as Killeith, and still earlier as Kildeleth (Kil=church), and we read of copper mining in the 17th century on the estate of Killeith, which does not seem to have been very productive. Continuing past Mid Kinleith Farm, the route from Currie to Glencorse by Kirkgate is joined in a quarter mile at

"Crossroads", which was at one time a smithy before conversion into the present dwelling house.

A shorter way from Woodhall Road at Colinton to East Kinleith is to go up Torphin Road to Torphin golf course (the bus terminus) and the quarry, from which a track, an old drove road, goes along the north slope of Torphin Hill to East Kinleith. This track reaches a height of 800 feet—almost the height of Arthur's Seat—and provides a fine panorama of Edinburgh and the Firth of Forth.

From the "Crossroads" on the Kirkgate a road continues south-west past West Kinleith and Harlaw Farms to Malleny Mills and Balerno. There is an alternative, if slightly longer, route by turning off the road at Harlaw Farm and making for the waterman's house at the reservoir, then walking by the path alongside Harlaw and Threipmuir Reservoirs to join the Bavelaw Castle road above Marchbank, from which it is a mile downhill to the top of Balerno village.

5. Route 5—Colinton by Howden Glen to Flotterstone 5 Miles

Dreghorn—"Covenanters' Monument"—Braid Burn—Howden Glen—Reindeer Cave—Allermuir—Castlelaw Fort—Crosshouse.

THIS route from Howden Glen over the hill to Castlelaw is on military ground and access is restricted to days when the firing range at Dreghorn is not in use; for this information consult the Ranger Service Information Centre at Hillend Park (Tel. 445 3383).

The first part of this walk is open to the public at all times, either starting from Colinton by Dreghorn Loan, or from Fairmilehead by Hunter's Tryst, to Dreghorn Mains. Between Dreghorn Loan and Redford Road the Braid Burn runs a picturesque course through the wooded grounds of the former Dreghorn Castle, now demolished after the War Office took over the whole estate for a training ground. The Castle was built in the 17th century by Sir William Murray, Master of the Works to Charles II, who came into possession of the property on marrying a daughter of Sir James Foulis of Colinton. In the early 18th century it was owned by the Pitcairns, a family derived from Principal Alexander Pitcairn of St. Andrews, grandson of the sixteenth Pitcairn of that Ilk. As the inscription in Colinton Churchyard records, from this branch were descended, among a host of other distinguished persons, Dr. Robertson, the historian, and Lord Brougham. George Home of Kelloe became the owner in 1720 and had for many years as a tutor to his family David Malloch, the author of *William and Margaret*, a ballad composed by him as he wandered on the banks of the Braid Burn. This and other poems brought him fame; he moved to London, where he changed his name to Mallet, and continued his poetical work.

About 1762, John Maclaurin, son of Professor Maclaurin of the Mathematical Chair in Edinburgh University, bought the property with the proceeds of the sale of his paternal estate of Drygrange, in Roxburghshire. He was a Member of the Faculty of Advocates, and being raised to the Bench in the year 1788, assumed the title of Lord Dreghorn.

"COVENANTERS MONUMENT"

His eldest son, Colin Maclaurin, sold the estate within a year of his father's death to Mr. Alexander Trotter of the "Bush" family. It came, in 1862, by purchase, into the hands of R. A. Macfie, sometime M.P. for the Leith Burghs, who erected the tall monument in Redford Road which has on its four sides at the top "Romans",

"Cromwell 1650", "Covenanters 1666", and "Charles 1745". The pillars of this monument originally formed the colonnade in front of the old Royal Infirmary, Edinburgh.

Close by is a picturesque scene where the old bridge spans the Braid Burn. Fine examples of fir and beech are all around, rising out of dense underwood, from which the rhododendrons blaze out in colour in due season. Snowberry there is also, and a wealth of primroses in their time. The place is a paradise for singing birds, the cuckoo being heard in its season, and the stream is rippled and circled by the movements of water hens, which rest there.

Howden Glen and the "Reindeer Cave"

At the bend in the road behind Dreghorn, where the road up Dreghorn Loan meets the road from Hunter's Tryst, a signpost "Bonaly : Kirkton : Castlelaw" marks the way across a field to the corner of the woods on the left. Here one track goes steeply uphill on the way to Bonaly Reservoir; for Howden Glen go through a gate and then uphill by a broad track. The direction ahead to Howden Glen is clear; shortly the path descends to the Green Craig Cistern, on which is its date, 1790, and the name Thomas Elder, Lord Provost at that time. High up on the hill on the left can be seen the fissure in the rock which was named the "Reindeer Cave", where in 1886 mammalian remains were found. It was reported that the remains contained bones of the horse, wolf, and fox, but the greater number were those of the reindeer, and represented parts of at least five individuals of that species. The condition of the bones and their environment seemed to show that they constituted part of the contents of the lair of some large carnivora, for they were gnawed and split up in the manner characteristic of the bones of the prey of such carnivora as the hyena. The rock fissure where the bones were found was cut out of a vein containing a large percentage of lime, and some of the bones, along with fragments of rocks, were cemented together with lime. Others lay loose among the weathered rock that filled the fissure. The fissure was not like a rut cut out by water from the hill, but resembled the well-known fissure at Salisbury Crags termed the "Cat Nick", and was thought to have been cut out in the rock after the ice of the glacial period had left the district, and when little or no vegetation existed on the hill, and that the carnivorous animals had taken possession before the refilling process had long commenced, as all the bones occupied a position near the bottom. It was remarked that the finding of these bones was by far the most important discovery yet made as to the existence of reindeer in Scotland. There is nothing now to be seen on the spot save the rift in the hill.

Allermuir

The track now crosses the Howden Burn, and then as a broad grassy path begins the climb up the glen, quite a steep ascent. At the top a track crossing the path leads on the left to Allermuir (1619 feet), from whose summit there is an even more extensive view than from Caerketton, the eye ranging from Cheviot over the Moorfoots to the Highland hills on the northern horizon, all Edinburgh spread out on the plain below. As we continue along the path a splendid view opens up ahead of the Pentland ridge from Turnhouse Hill to the Kips, with the two reservoirs, Glencorse and Loganlee, like lochs in a deep glen, making this one of the finest views in the Pentlands. At a point where the dike coming down from Allermuir is met the grassy path ends and is succeeded by a rough roadway used by tractors. As this crosses Fala Knowe we look down on the towns and villages of the valley of the Esk and over them to the Moorfoots; the view becoming ever more extensive as the track swings round the eastern slope of Castlelaw Hill and, now that Caerketton is behind, gives a panorama extending from the Bass Rock along the Lammermuir and Moorfoot Hills to the distant hills of Peeblesshire and of Upper Clydesdale.

Castlelaw Fort

Just before Castlelaw Farm is reached the path skirts Castle Knowe, a knoll on which is a series of earthen ramparts where excavations in 1931/32 unexpectedly revealed a souterrain or earth house. The description reads: "This iron age fortified settlement is defended by three ramparts and ditches. Excavation has demonstrated that the two outer lines of defence were an addition to a single rampart and ditch which itself was preceded by a timber palisade. These three phases all date to the last centuries B.C. The fort was probably abandoned in the Roman period when a souterrain was constructed in one of the ditches. Such underground passages or chambers are widely distributed in Scotland. Their function is uncertain—dwellings, storehouses, workshops, byres and hiding places are all possible explanations." The interior consists of a passage some 76 feet in length, from 3 to 6½ feet wide, with walls 4 to 5 feet in height lined with masonry composed of boulders and large stones. Midway along the passage a branch opens into a roughly circular annex. The key for this interesting place can be obtained at the farm of Crosshouse down on the Biggar road, to which a road descends from Castlelaw Farm. Without the key a length of the passage can be seen from the entrance gate.

From Crosshouse it is half a mile to Flotterstone, or just over a mile by Glencorse Old Kirk to Milton Bridge.

6. Route 6—Colinton by Bonaly to Flotterstone and Glencorse 5 Miles

Bonaly Tower—Lord Cockburn on Bonaly—View from Bonaly Tower—A Meeting of the Faithful at Bonaly—Professor Blackie on Bonaly Burn—A Pawky Pentland Shepherd—Lord Cockburn's Fruitful Suggestion—Hugh Miller on Glencorse—Story of the Hunt of Pentland—St. Catherine's Chapel—Edinburgh Water Supply—The Reservoirs.

THIS route from Colinton to Glencorse by Bonaly, being so accessible from town, is one of the most popular walks on the Pentlands. The return can be made in many ways—to Currie, by Loganlee to Balerno, or by the Biggar road and Hillend to Fairmilehead.

From Woodhall Road at Colinton, Bonaly Road strikes up to the foot of the hills. There appears to have been a village of Bonaly to the west of Bonaly Tower in the year 1652. There were waulk-mills worked by the water power of Bonaly Burn, a distillery, skinnery, and magnesia manufactory, and dwelling-houses, of course, but they have all disappeared. Originally a farmhouse, Lord Cockburn altered it in 1845, and since that time it has had further additions, making it the imposing building we now see. It has now been converted into flats. There is an excellent description of the place, its outlook, and the approach to it, in Meiklejohn's *Life of Professor Hodgson*, who lived there from 1874 to 1880. We give Meiklejohn's account here:—

"Striking south for the Pentlands, right for the heart of the lovely hills, he finds the road constantly rising, and the view at every step becomes wider. Suddenly at its highest point, the road dips again, and before him appears a round tower rising out of a thick mass of trees, and flanked on the right by crags and steeply escarped hills, and where the eye turns to the left, far away across the southern suburbs of Edinburgh, stands the lion form of Arthur's Seat, with the Crags of Salisbury stretching from its base. Turning and looking North, he sees the noble sea-breadth of the Firth of Forth and the rich shores of the ancient 'Kingdom of Fife'. This ground on which Bonaly Tower stands seems only a narrow nook, but as you go down, it broadens into a fair garden and broad-spread grounds, thick with beeches, sycamores, pines and evergreens; a clear mountain burn rushing through the grounds, and the song of birds in every corner. Massive hills shut in the garden from cold and boisterous winds, and a long winding path edged with flower-beds, running along the stream, leads you to the grassy sides of the main range of the Pentland Hills."

Lord Cockburn on Bonaly

Bonaly Tower is a singularly picturesque building, exhibiting the charming variety of round and square outlines, hanging turrets and conical roofs which belong to the Scotch castellated style. It owes its existence to Lord Cockburn, by whom it is thus described in his *Memorials*. "In March 1811 I married, and set up my rural household gods at Bonaly, in the parish of Colinton, close by the northern base of the Pentland Hills; and unless some avenging angel shall expel me, I shall never leave that paradise. I began by an annual lease of a few square yards and a scarcely habitable farm house. But realising the profanations of Auburn, I have destroyed a village and erected a tower, and reached the dignity of a twenty-acred laird. Everything except the two burns, the few old trees, and the mountains, is my own work, and to a great extent the work of my own hands. Human nature is incapable of enjoying more happiness than has been my lot here, where the glories of the prospects, and the luxury of the wild retirement, have been all enhanced by the progress of my improvements, of my children and of myself. I have been too happy, and often tremble in the anticipation that the cloud must come at last. Warburton says there was not a bush in his garden on which he had not hung a speculation. There is not a recess in the valleys of the Pentlands, nor an eminence on their summits, that is not familiar to my solitude. One summer I read every word of Tacitus in the sheltered crevice of a rock (called 'My Seat'), about 800 feet above the level of the sea, with the most magnificent of scenes before me".

View from Bonaly Tower

The view from Bonaly Tower is thus described; even finer is the view from the path up the hill.

"If we go to the top of the tower, and out upon the roof of the main building, we shall have before us a view such as is seldom to be seen, even in Scotland. The eye has a range of at least eighty miles, and takes in highlands and lowlands, town and country. The distant peaks of the Perthshire Grampians; the higher mountains of the Trossachs, Ben Ledi, Ben Lomond, Ben A'an; the green rounded masses of the Ochils; the level valley of the winding Forth; the escarpment of the table-land of Kinross; the twin Lomonds of Fife; nearer the gentle wooded heights of Corstorphine; the mighty belt of the great sea-river; the solitary Arthur's Seat; the conical Berwick Law; the stumpy mass of the Bass Rock; the regular streets of

Edinburgh, broken into by the rugged hump of Craiglockhart—all this and more the eye takes in with ease and delight. There are few landscapes more beautiful or more varied. Eight counties—Perthshire, Stirlingshire, Clackmannan, Kinross, Fife, the three Lothians—fall into it".

A Meeting of the Faithful at Bonaly

There was in existence in 1842 a "Bonaly Friday Club", with three dozen members, many of them afterwards known to fame who enjoyed themselves here.

Lord Cockburn, in the autumn of 1853, invited James Nasmyth, of steam-hammer fame, to have a "hill day" at Bonaly, and to bring "the faithful" with him. These included his wife, David Roberts, Clarkson Stanfield, Louis and Carl Haag, Sir George Harvey, James Ballantine and D. O. Hill, all artists. "We made our way", writes Nasmyth, "to bonny Bonaly, a charming residence, situated at the foot of the Pentland Hills. The day was perfect, in all respects 'equal to bespoke'. With the most genial of men, Lord Cockburn, for our guide, we wandered far up the Pentland Hills. After a rather toilsome walk, we reached a favourite spot. It was a semi-circular hollow in the hillside, scooped out by the sheep for shelter. It was carpeted and cushioned with a deep bed of wild thyme, redolent of the very essence of rural fragrance. We sat down in a semi-circle, our guide in the middle. He said in his quaint, peculiar way, 'Here endeth the first lesson'. After gathering our breath, and settling ourselves to enjoy our well-earned rest, we sat in silence for a time. The gentle breeze blew past us, and we inhaled the fragrant air. It was enough for a time to look on, for the glorious old city was before us, with its towers, and spires, and lofty buildings between us and the distance. On one side Arthur's Seat, and on the other the Castle, the crown of the city. The view extended far and wide on to the waters of the Forth, and the blue hills of Fife. The view is splendidly described by David Macbeth Moir:

Traced like a map, the landscape lies
In cultured beauty, stretching wide:
Here Pentland's green acclivities,
There ocean, with its swelling tide,
There Arthur's Seat, and, gleaming through
Thy southern wing, Dun Edin blue!
While in the Orient, Lammer's daughters,
A distant giant range, are seen;
North Berwick Law with cone of green,
And Bass amid the waters."

There was haggis on the bill of fare at Bonaly that day, and the host, master in the art of conversation, was quick, ready, and full of wit.

Professor Blackie and Bonaly Burn

Professor Blackie, poet and scholar, wrote on the mountain burn which runs through the grounds. Here we quote only the last two verses.

Come with the memory, pleasant and sweet,
Of the mellow-souled judge, for his leafy retreat,
Who trimmed the old tower of Bonaly;
Whose heart was as kind as the old grass that grows,
Whose voice was as sweet as the water that flows
Round the green ivy-tower of Bonaly.

Come with bright thoughts like my fountain that wells
Round the grey-castled hall where the wise thinker dwells
By the quiet green slope of the valley;
And bathe thee in seas of the flowery perfume
That floats from the breath of the furze and the broom,
By the bonnie green burn o' Bonaly.

A Pawky Pentland Shepherd

To Grahame, the author of the poem *The Sabbath*, this was a favourite resort. Lord Rutherford has the following story told of him by Dean Ramsay, how he was rebuked by a shepherd, near Bonaly. He had entered into conversation with him, and was complaining bitterly of the weather, which prevented him enjoying his visit to the country, and said hastily, and unguardedly, 'What a d—d mist!' and then expressed his wonder how or for what purpose there should have been such a thing created as east wind. The shepherd, a tall, grim figure, turned sharply round upon him, "What ails ye at the mist, sir? it weets the sod, it slockens the yowes, and forbye", adding with much solemnity, "it's God's wull". Lord Cockburn himself was called to account, though for a more venial transgression. He was sitting on the hillside with the shepherd, and observing the sheep reposing in the coldest situation, he said to him, "John, if I were a sheep, I would lie on the other side of the hill". The shepherd replied, "Ay, my lord, but if ye had been a sheep, ye wad hae had mair sense".

Lord Cockburn's Fruitful Suggestion

According to Principal Shairp, the idea of the Edinburgh Academy suggested itself to Lord Cockburn as he trod the top of one of the

Pentland hills. "On the top of one of the Pentlands, the idea of a new classical school (the Edinburgh Academy) first flashed on the brain of Henry, Lord Cockburn. It was a fitting birthplace for a large and beneficent idea. Not in the retirement of the lawyer's study, not under his wig in the Parliament House, but under his rustic hat, with the free Pentland winds blowing about his manly and expressive face, that idea was born".

But we pass from Bonaly upwards through the public recreation ground on the lower slope of the hill, and towards Glencorse along the old bridle road. The myriads of pedestrians who have gone that way, who can recount?—amongst them Professor Playfair and Lord Webb Seymour. Lord Cockburn used to envy them their Pentland walks together. Numerous, no doubt, in the middle ages, the path is still marked by streams of goers and comers during the season; nor is it solitary on this route in winter or uninspiring at that time, as may be seen from the verses by Will H. Ogilvie given on the back of the title page.

It is from the ascent to Bonaly Reservoir that the "lion, splendidly sleeping, and the tall crags silent and grey", are seen to the east. At the summit of the watershed is a stile, which crossed discloses a descending path to Glencorse valley, whence we have a distant view of the Esk ravine, with the hills behind. On the left, up the Capelaw hollow, are the slight remains of a former croft; on the right, further down, up the Loganlee valley, the Kips come into sight, with Scald Law bounding the view.

Hugh Miller on Glencorse

No one who has been alone in the heart of the hills here can forget the haunting charm of Castlelaw, Carnethy, or the Logan burn twinkling down the vale from Loganlee. Glencorse reservoir is an artificial loch receiving the Logan and Kirk burns, the Glencorse burn issuing at the other end of it. It was formed in 1822 as an equivalent for the loss of water sustained by the water mills on the Esk, and also for an addition to the water supply of Edinburgh. Of Glencorse Reservoir Hugh Miller writes: "People at a distance, when they hear Glencorse Reservoir called a Compensation Pond, might imagine it little superior to a tolerable horse one, with a submerged churchyard at its bottom, infused for the special benefit of our Edinburgh water-drinkers. But not such the character of the Compensation Pond. Let the reader imagine of it as marked by all the better characteristics of a genuine Highland loch in a genuine Highland glen, surrounded by bold steep banks, embosomed by hills varying from a thousand to nineteen hundred feet in height, with water much more than enough . . . Were an ordinary sized sloop to founder in some of the deepest parts of the Compensation Pond, the whole of the mainmast would disappear, and two-thirds of the topmast to boot".

Story of the Hunt of Pentland

Sir Walter Scott, in a note to the *Lay of the Last Minstrel*, thus relates the story of the founding of St. Catherine's. "King Robert the Bruce following the chase upon Pentland Hills, had often started a 'white faunch deer', which had always escaped from his hounds; and he asked the nobles, who were assembled around him, whether any of them had dogs which they thought might be more successful. No courtier would affirm that his hounds were fleeter than those of the King, until Sir William St. Clair of Roslin unceremoniously said he would wager his head that his two favourite dogs, Help and Hold, would kill the deer before she would cross the March-burn. The King instantly caught at his unwary offer, and betted the forest of Pentlandmoor against the life of Sir William St. Clair. All the hounds were tied up, except a few ratches, or slow-hounds, to put up the deer; while Sir William St. Clair posting himself at the best situation for slipping his dogs, prayed devoutly to Christ, the blessed Virgin, and St. Catherine. The deer was shortly after roused and the hounds slipped, Sir William following on a gallant steed, to cheer his dogs. The hind, however, reached the middle of the brook, at which the hunter threw himself from his horse in despair. At this critical moment, Hold stopped her in the brook; and Help, coming up, turned her back, and killed her on St. William's side. The King descended from the hill, embraced Sir William, and bestowed on him the lands of Kirkton, Loganhouse, Earncraig, etc., in free forestrie. Sir William, in acknowledgment of St. Catherine's intercession, built the chapel of St. Catherine in the Hopes. The hill, from which Robert Bruce beheld this memorable chase, is still called the King's Hill; and the place where Sir William hunted, is called the Knight's Field". King's Hill is behind Kirkton Farm and Knightfield Rig is where the Bonaly path descends to Glencorse Reservoir. Sir William St. Clair was one of the band of Scottish Knights who set off with Sir James Douglas to carry the heart of Robert Bruce to the Holy Land; both were slain by the Saracens in Spain in 1330.

St. Catherine's Chapel

The formation of Glencorse Reservoir necessitated the submergence of St. Catherine's Chapel, the foundations of which have been several times exposed in dry years, having been observed last in 1972. The fragment of wall that remains indicates that the chapel was about 44 feet long and 20 feet wide, standing due east and west. It is said that when the Chapel was submerged the graveyard was fully a quarter of an acre in extent, and the boundary wall visible about 12 inches above the ground; the Logan burn running 20 yards south of the south boundary wall (remains of this wall may still be seen in a dry season about 20 yards south of the Chapel), and the March burn 20 yards east. Only a heap of stones remains.

The Chapel is referred to as existing in 1230, Henry de Brade making a gift in that year of the teinds from the lands of Bavelaw Castle to the monks of Holyrood for the support of the chapel of St. Catherine of the Pentlands. It was annexed to the bishopric of Edinburgh, and added to Penicuik in 1635. It was named St. Catherine of the Hopes ("hope" being a hollow among hills), probably in distinction to St. Catherine's upon the Hill, at the Balm Well, near Liberton.

Edinburgh Water Supply

Edinburgh water supply originally came from draw-wells in the city, which in time became contaminated with sewage and too limited in quantity. The wells were thereafter supplemented by water from the South Loch, where are now the Meadows, according to a resolution made in 1598. By 1681, as mentioned in Route 1, Edinburgh had secured a supply from Comiston Springs. Forty years later other springs were added and land purchased for the collection of the Swanston springs.

When the New Town was being built, new springs were acquired at Bonaly and an installation formed in 1822, at Crawley and Glencorse. Telford and Rennie, the celebrated engineers, were responsible for the plans. The Bonaly ponds were afterwards abandoned; their site may be noticed on the left hand of the ascent to Bonaly Reservoir.

The Reservoirs

In 1848, the Black Springs and those of Bavelaw and Liston Shiels were available, and Threipmuir and Harlaw in 1847q48, as compensation to the mill owners on the Bavelaw Burn and Water of Leith. Clubbiedean (1850), Torduff (1851), Loganlee (1851), and Bonaly (1853), were added, and in 1859, the Colzium Springs, at the source of the Water of Leith, were gathered into the Harperrig Reservoir, partly as compensation and partly as city supply; then, in 1868, came the absorption of the Crosswood springs and the formation of the Crosswood Reservoir.

In 1869 the Edinburgh and District Water Trust took the place of the old water authorities, and secured the springs which formed the Gladhouse Reservoir, at the foot of the Moorfoot Hills. In the distant Talla valley, Peeblesshire, a reservoir, two miles long, was formed to provide an additional supply to the city in 1905, and supplemented in more recent years by the water from the Fruid Reservoir. The water supply is now controlled by Lothian Region Water Supply Service.

Return may be made by road (4 miles to Fairmilehead), by bus or by Route No. 5 reversed. From Flotterstone it is 1½ miles by Glencorse Old Kirk to the Fisher's Tryst Inn at Milton Bridge.

7. Route 7—Currie or Balerno to Flotterstone 5 Miles

(a) Currie—Kirkgate—Maiden's Cleuch—Glencorse.
(b) Balerno—Harlaw.

(a) *From Currie*

Currie Bridge and Currie Church are described in Route 4. The road from Currie to the hills, by the Kirkgate, rises steeply from 500 feet at the church to 757 feet at the house at Kinleith "Cross-roads". The remainder of the five miles to Flotterstone is pleasant walking. At the end of Whiteside plantation the track comes out on the open moor, where at one time the Army had a shooting range on the left. On the right can be seen Harlaw Reservoir and soon the path is joined by the right of way from Balerno. Hunting and poaching were long practised here. R. B. Langwill, in his notes on Currie Parish, mentions that six persons of this parish had to appear before the Privy Council for poaching on the Pentlands. They belonged to Whelpside, Riccarton, Warriston and Currie, and were all convicted, when they were obliged to promise that none of their children, tenants, nor servants should, for all time coming, hunt with their dogs within the space of six miles of His Majesty's Castle of Edinburgh. Neither were they to keep hounds or dogs upon any condition whatever. Lennox Tower, Baberton and Bavelaw, are traditional hunting seats of James VI.

Maiden's Cleuch

It was up the Kirkgate from Currie and through Maiden's Cleuch, between Harbour Hill on the left and Bell's Hill on the right, that Dalziel of Binns rode towards Rullion Green (Route 2). This was of old the drove road to House o' Muir market held just south of Flotterstone, and at several places on the route one can see the old road running parallel with the path, both on the approach to the pass and on the left going down towards Glencorse Reservoir. Dr. Jamieson, writing in 1845, calls Maiden's Cleuch, Cleuchmaidstone, as being the pass to the Chapel of St. Catherine, Glencorse, and having a font of water, in which the pilgrims washed before entering the Chapel of the Holy Maid of St. Catherine.

Beyond Maiden's Cleuch the path descends, and just short of Glencorse Reservoir joins the path from Colinton by Bonaly (see Route 6 for Glencorse Reservoir and St. Catherine's). On the other side of Glencorse Reservoir part of the old road going over to House o' Muir can be seen on the hillside rising from the reservoir. From

Flotterstone the walk may be continued by Glencorse Old Kirk to Milton Bridge, or by Easter Howgate to Hillend and Fairmilehead.

(b) *From Balerno*

Just beyond the paper mill at the upper end of the old village of Balerno, Harlaw Road goes left: it crosses the Bavelaw Burn and then passes some houses built by the paper mill company for their workers. Higher up, on the right, in the valley, are the various buildings still called Malleny Mills, although no mill now operates. Where the road takes a left turn to Harlaw Farm you have two options: (a) continue along the road to the farm and there turn right by a road which leads to a gate and a signpost pointing the way to Glencorse, or (b) follow the path up the bank of the Bavelaw Burn to the waterman's house and here turn left along a road to the signpost. From this point you cross a field and the moor to join, in less than a mile, the path coming from Currie by the Kirkgate.

8. Route 8—Balerno by Loganlee to Penicuik or Flotterstone 8 Miles

Balerno to Glencorse—Threipmuir—Bavelaw—Kirk Road to Penicuik—Loganlee and the Howlet's House—Logan Tower.

No Pentland walk is finer than this, passing as it does through such varied scenery of hill, glen and loch (as the reservoirs might well be called), that one could be a hundred miles from the city. Even the steady stream of walkers to be seen at week-ends going towards the hills from the straggling village of Balerno gets so scattered on the hills that the solitude of many parts is never disturbed. Above the older part of Balerno village, whose old main street is no longer a through route for vehicles, the road divides; the higher road going direct to Bavelaw, and the lower one, Harlaw Road, branching left immediately past the paper mill, the mainstay of Balerno employment for a century and a half until paper making ceased some years ago. The lower road goes up by Malleny Mills, old buildings on the Bavelaw Burn surviving from the days when part of them was once a spinning mill and part once a grain mill. Where the road bends left to Harlaw Farm a path goes up the bank of the burn to Harlaw Reservoir in its picturesque setting of fir trees. Beyond the waterman's house we cross the embankment and follow the track round the reservoir and then along by the side of Threipmuir Reservoir until it joins the direct road coming up from Balerno by Whinrig and Marchbank. On the west side of this road is the Red Moss Wildlife Reserve of the Scottish Wildlife Trust. This walk by the reservoirs is the more attractive approach to Bavelaw, but the quicker approach is by the bus route (the upper road from the paper mill) up to the higher end of the housing scheme, which leaves only a mile to walk to Marchbank.

Threipmuir

The name of Threipmuir, according to the old story already quoted, arose when Sir William St. Clair, of Roslin, staked his head against his hounds, when hunting with King Robert the Bruce, and threeped the dogs in pursuit of a white deer. The notes of encouragement were successful; St. Clair's head remained on his shoulders; he received a grant of the forest of Pentland from the King, and in gratitude, founded the Chapel of St. Catherine of the Hopes at Glencorse. Threipmuir and Harlaw are compensation ponds, and the former has been raised to meet the needs of the Water of Leith purification scheme.

Beside the bridge over Threipmuir are the ruins of Redford, which, according to tradition, were the hunting stables of James VI. James VI also hunted around Bavelaw, and Queen Mary came up from Lennox Tower on the Water of Leith, to hawk here.

Bavelaw

A pleasant avenue, which has been well called the Gate of the Pentlands, leads past Bavelaw Castle, the teinds on the land of which were given by Henry de Brade, during the reign of William the Lion, in favour of the monks of Holyrood, for the support of St. Catherine's of the Pentlands. In the course of changes of ownership, the castle came into the possession of Robert Mowbray of Barnbougle in the 16th century, and in 1628 the King granted it to Laurence Scott of Harperrig, one of a younger branch of the Malleny Scotts, already referred to; and, later, in 1783, the castle came into the hands of the Johnstones, merchants of Gothenburg. The present building is mainly of 17th century construction; in 1628, Scott complained to the Privy Council that four men had gone to Bavelaw, where he had just built two turrets and covered them with lead, and "rave doun and tooke away with thame the most pairt of the leid being upon the said turrets for the making of bullets to their hacquebutts".

From Bavelaw the path, bearing to the left, makes for the Green Cleuch, the narrow pass between Hare Hill and the dark mass of Black Hill. As the cleuch widens out, the Logan Burn comes in on the right, forming in its descent from the heights a high and picturesque waterfall. Few spots in the Pentlands are more popular with picnic parties.

Kirk Road to Penicuik

The ascent by the Kirk Road for Penicuik is made from Logan Burn, above Loganlee Cottage, and is marked by posts. Bavelaw and the Logan Valley are both in the parish of Penicuik, and this was their road to the church of Penicuik. The watershed is crossed between Carnethy and Scald Law, at 1456 feet. A climb of twenty minutes from here will take the walker to the summit of Scald Law (1899 feet), the highest point of the Pentlands. After descending the Grain Burn, the Biggar road is reached, east of Silverburn. For Penicuik turn left towards Edinburgh and take the first road on the right by Coates; on reaching the housing scheme continue downhill to the main road (A766).

Loganlee and the Howlet's House

If, instead of crossing the hill to the Biggar road, we take the easier alternative of going by the reservoirs to Flotterstone, we have a road all the way. On an eminence overlooking a burn flowing into Loganlee Reservoir is the ruin of a building, dating probably from the end of the 16th century, popularly called the "Howlet's House", but most likely the priests' manse belonging to St. Catherine's Chapel of the Hollow, with its own chapel attached. Part of one of the vaulted roofs remains, with some of the original plaster upon it. This vault was complete in 1877. It is to be hoped that what still remains will be preserved. The ruin is charmingly situated on the rocky bank, and looks down on an undergrowth of bushes with rowan trees, which margin the streamlet on its northern side.

Logan Tower

Half a mile below Loganlee Reservoir is Logan House, where once stood Logan Tower, an ancient keep which belonged to the St. Clairs of Roslin from very early times. It has been demolished and the few stones which have survived need not detain the passer-by. In 1681 Logan House and Kirkton lands, with tower and fortalice, passed by purchase from the St. Clairs to Alexander Gibson. In 1782, they came into possession of William Ferguson of Raith, and in 1831, of William Robertson, who sold them to Charles Gowan, M.P., about 1852.

At Loganlee we are three miles from Flotterstone and below the shadow of Carnethy, and face Castlelaw which blocks the valley to the eastward. The road winds pleasantly and deviously past Glencorse Reservoir to Flotterstone Bridge. If we continue back to town, twelve miles will have been covered since leaving Balerno.

9. Route 9—Balerno to Nine Mile Burn 6 Miles

Bavelaw—Kitchen Moss—West Kip and Eastside—Monks Road —G. M. Kemp—Newhall—Allan Ramsay—*The Gentle Shepherd.*

ROUTE 9, between Balerno and Nine-Mile-Burn, is the same as Route 8 as far as Bavelaw, where the path divides, the one to the left leading to Loganlee (Route 8). We follow the one to the right, which climbs over the south-west shoulder of Hare Hill at a height of 1322 feet, and then crosses Kitchen Moss, the source of the Logan Burn. In approaching the watershed at the base of West Kip, the view eastward of Castlelaw, Carnethy and Scald Law is very fine.

WEST KIP AND EASTSIDE

From the watershed it is an easy climb to West Kip (1806 feet), which, though not the highest of the Pentland Hills—Scald Law, 1899 feet; Carnethy, 1890 feet; West Cairn, 1844 feet; and East Cairn Hill, 1839 feet, are all higher—is the most outstanding, its graceful tapering peak being a feature in the view looking up the Loganlee valley from Glencorse Reservoir, or from Allermuir Hill. The top of West Kip is really a narrow rocky ridge. East Kip is close by, only 55 feet lower. On the watershed the path divides into three; the left-hand branch by Eastside taking the shortest way to the Biggar road, passing, about a third of a mile short of the road, the hill fort on Camp Hill. The fort is 232 feet in length, and 175 feet in breadth; its defences, consisting of an inner ditch, a rampart of stone and earth, and a second ditch, are still well preserved. To reach Penicuik from here one must go left for half a mile to Silverburn, from which it is two miles to Penicuik main street.

MONKS ROAD

From the ridge at East Kip there is a choice of two routes to Nine Mile Burn. One path goes downhill along the south slope of the valley, and then strikes to the right over Braid Law, its line clearly defined by posts down to Nine Mile Burn. A more interesting route is to turn to the right at the ridge along a path which ascends over Cap Law and just beyond the summit passes the Font Stone, a rectangular stone 3 feet 2 inches in height, with a hollow on the top, probably the socket of an ancient cross, which may have marked the pilgrimage way between the monastery (which stood at Newhall) and Queensferry. In 1835 some old copper coins were found under the socket of the cross. To the south, on the other side of the Monks Burn, is the farm of Spittal, believed to be on the site of the old hospice, an outpost of the monastery, which wayfarers used to visit for supper and a night's accommodation, as monastic usage led them to expect. It is only right to admit that there is neither documentary nor architectural evidence to prove there was a monastery at Newhall. But the names, Monks Rig, Monks Road, Monks Burn, Monks Haugh, and Friarton, and also the farm called Spittal, are strong evidence in favour of such occupation. The inn at Nine Mile Burn is on the old coach road to Biggar, described in a later chapter. Nine Mile Burn is nine Scots miles from Edinburgh; many a traveller from England in the old days complained of the long Scots miles.

G. M. Kemp

George Meikle Kemp was an infant when his father, a Biggar shepherd, came to live on the Newhall Estate, at Nine Mile Burn. Being sent on one occasion on a message to Roslin by Mr. Brown, of Newhall, in his tenth year (1806), he seems to have received the impression that determined his future calling. The history of his career is well known, and it is interesting to recall his meeting in the valley of the Tweed with Sir Walter Scott, who invited him to a seat in his carriage, and drove him to Galashiels, Sir Walter enthusiastically describing the Border ecclesiastical antiquities to one who was to design the monument in Princes Street, which Professor Mason said was one of the finest ever erected to a man of genius.

Newhall

The lands of Newhall were granted by Robert III, early in 1400, to Laurence Creichtoune, and his descendants held them till the beginning of the 17th century. Dr. Alexander Pennecuik acquired Newhall in 1656; his son Alexander was author of a *Description of Tweeddale.* In 1703 it became the property of Sir David Forbes of the Culloden family. In the beginning of the 18th century most of the old place was pulled down by the then possessor, John Forbes, an advocate, and the present house built by him. It was the popular resort, in Mr. Forbes' day, of many of the leading literary men, among whom was Allan Ramsay, whose poem, *The Gentle Shepherd,* was published in 1725. Of the various places suggested as the scene of the poem, Newhall has the strongest claim as the spot "where a' the sweets o' spring and summer grow", and where runs the "trotting burnie wimpling through the ground".

One of the later proprietors, Hugh Horatio Brown, did much to beautify the grounds and identify the place with the scenes in *The Gentle Shepherd.* In the library at Newhall there is a painted ceiling showing Allan Ramsay and his brother worthies.

SCENERY OF *The Gentle Shepherd*

An illustrated booklet published last century furnishes views of this neighbourhood identifying it at every turn with Allan Ramsay's *Gentle Shepherd.* There is a portrait of Allan Ramsay in the front, with nose elongated as much as is the case in Captain Elliot's sketch of the poet John Leyden. The views include the Fore Spital of Newhall, with the Pentlands behind; Newhall House, with a distant view of Simon's Farm; Habbie's Howe; Linn Burn; Washing Green behind Newhall House, with maidens near a wash-tub:

A flowery howme between twa verdant braes,
Where lasses used to wash and spread their claes,
A trotting burnie, wimpling through the ground.
Its channel pebbles shining smooth and round.

Then there are Glaud's farm and entrance to Habbie's Howe, with the motto:

Gae farer up the burn to Habbie's Howe,
Where a' that's sweet in spring and summer grow.

Next are Habbie's Howe from the Washing Green; Harbour Craig, 1 mile south-east of Newhall, associated with Covenanting gatherings; Upper Linn of Monks Burn behind Glaud's Farm; Mause's Cottage and Roger's Habitation above Habbie's Howe; Simon's Cottage over the Esk, from Marfield Loch, with Carlops Hill in the distance. These were to illustrate an edition of *The Gentle Shepherd,* with Illustrations of the Scenery, believed to be edited by R. D. C. Brown of Newhall. The whole topography of the district in connection with the *Gentle Shepherd* is discussed, and the scenery described. Edinburgh has had its monument to the poet for many years. Sir James Clerk erected in 1759 a memorial with inscription in the grounds of Penicuik House. Tytler says: "When I passed my infancy at Newhall, near Pentland Hills, where the scene of this pastoral poem was laid, the seat of Mr. Forbes, and the resort of many of the *literati* at that time, I well remember to have heard Ramsay recite as his own production different scenes of the *Gentle Shepherd,* particularly the two first, before it was printed".

Penicuik is 4½ miles from Nine Mile Burn.

10. Route 10—Balerno to Carlops 9 Miles

Traces of the Templars—Listonshiels—The Bore Stane—North Esk Reservoir—Carlops—Harbour Craig.

FROM Balerno to Carlops by the Bore Stane is nine miles. Starting from the bus terminus at Balerno there is first a walk of two miles up the road to Marchbank and then, turning right here, along the road past East Rigg Farm. From the corner where the road turns left to West Rigg, the track of an old road continues straight ahead for another full mile to Listonshiels. The alternative, starting from Midcalder Station, is longer and less attractive as a walk; you have two miles of road up to the A70, and another half mile eastward along this busy highway to the road turning south past Haughhead Farm to Listonshiels. This road passes near Temple House, and to the west of Listonshiels is Temple Hill, reminders that the Templars at one time owned much of the land in this quarter. In fact, they had possessions in almost every county in Scotland. Sir James Sandilands, who built the choir of Mid Calder Church, was the last Grand Prior of the Hospitallers, and joined the Reformers in 1560. The Order was then suppressed, and Sir James, on paying a sum down, and engaging to pay an annual rent to the Crown, entered into possession of the remaining estates in that quarter as a temporal barony, and was created Lord Torphichen. Listonshiels was at one time attached to Kirkliston Church, and as its name implies, was probably a place where "shiels" had been erected for the shelter of the flocks and herds belonging to the patrimony of the Church.

BORE STANE

Beyond Listonshiels the path crosses the Bavelaw Burn and makes a steady climb to the Bore Stane, the name given to the outcrop of rocks beside some trees on the west of the path. The origin of the name seems to be unknown; certainly this spelling and not "Boar Stane" appears on old maps. At the summit of the pass we are 1300 feet above sea level and at the extreme northern point in the boundary of Peeblesshire and of the Borders Region. To the west is East Cairn Hill (1839 feet). The descent on the south down the valley of the River North Esk brings us in little over a mile to the North Esk Reservoir, constructed in 1846 by a private company to provide a regular supply of water for the mills on the banks of the Esk. Seven long graves on the islands in the reservoir were examined (1898), and described by J. W. Loney, and may have belonged to the early Christian period. A path crosses the end of the reservoir by the waterman's cottage and climbs over Spittal Hill to Spittal Farm and Nine Mile Burn. The road keeps on to Fairliehope Farm, where a post at the corner marks the start of the path which goes down the left bank of the North Esk to Carlops, an awkward path in the dark, but shorter than keeping to the road down to Carlops. The path is of a truly Highland character, until the old mill and the waterfall are reached, close to the Biggar road.

Carlops

The village of Carlops is of relatively modern origin, but the name is on record in the 14th century, when Andrew of Wyntoun in his *Orygynale Cronykle* describes "Karlynlippis" as being on the boundary of the lands between the Tweed and the Forth ceded by Edward Balliol to Edward III of England. The North Esk here marks the boundary between Peeblesshire (Borders Region) and Midlothian (Lothian Region). The name Karlynlippis or Carlops can, without much ingenuity, be read as "Carlin's Leap", to justify the story that a carline or witch is said to have lived in a dell at the foot of Carlops Hill, near a pass between two crags, and was often seen bounding across from the opposite points of these rocks on her broom. Modern quarrying and roadworks have greatly widened what was once a narrow passage between the two crags.

The owner of the lands of Carlops in 1715 was Archibald Burnet, who took part in the Jacobite rising in that year, was captured, and executed in Liverpool. In the 18th century Carlops consisted of a small mansion house and an inn, which may refer to the small farmhouse of Carlop Mains, a little east of the road at the "Carlin's Leap", said to have been originally an inn. In 1783 the estates of Carlops and Newhall were bought by Robert Brown, an advocate, who in the following year established a cotton weaving industry and built the attractive rows of weavers' cottages on each side of the main road. The Allan Ramsay Hotel has the date 1792 above the doorway. In 1800 a West Linton weaver, Alexander Alexander, built Patie's Mill in the gorge of the River Esk, as a woollen manufactory but this was short lived. It is a two-storeyed building now in use as a dwelling house beside the waterfall and bridge. On the Esk at Marfield was a flax mill, and further up a fulling mill and dyehouse. At Gladsheugh was a bleachfield, and near Marfield, a gunpowder mill, blown up in the year 1830, some of the workers, unhappily, being killed.

Harbour Craig

On the south of the River Esk about a mile east of Carlops is Harbour Craig, a great perpendicular rock rising to a height of 50 feet on the south side of the deep glen of the Back Burn close to its junction with the Harlawmuir Burn. According to tradition it was used as a gathering point for the local Covenanters and may have been used as a refuge on the retreat from Rullion Green. Several dates and names have been carved on the rock—1612, 1640, 1662, 1666, 1669—some now hardly decipherable; one of the names, J. Gifford, is the Laird Gifford associated with West Linton, which would support the tradition that he fought at Rullion Green. There are signs in the vicinity of the coal mining carried on here; the coal seam extends from Carlops through Harlawmuir, and was partially worked before the competition of cheaper coal brought by the railway.

11. Route 11—Mid Calder to West Linton by the Cauldstane Slap 12 Miles

Little Vantage—Colzium and Cairns—Cauldstane Slap—Baddinsgill—Cairnmuir—Bridgehouse—West Linton.

ROUTE No. 11 may be said to begin at Mid Calder, from which the starting point on the Lanark Road may be reached. Mid Calder itself has a very interesting old Parish Church, which is said to have been founded by Duncan, Earl of Fife, the then Lord of the Manor, in 1215, but there is no part of the church so old as that. From the Earls of Fife, from whom it had its old name of Earl's Calder, the Manor passed to the Douglasses and from them about the middle of the 14th century, to the knightly house of Sandilands. A younger son of the sixth Knight of Calder, and parson of the parish, laid the foundation of the choir, and raised the walls of the vestry before 1542. The transepts at the west end, which complete the church, are modern.

Ascending from the Calder valley, and after a three mile walk, we reach the Lanark Road, turn to the right for three quarters of a mile, passing the ruined inn called "Little Vantage", and then go southwards along the side of a fence towards the Cauldstane Slap. About a mile down we reach the Water of Leith, here a small stream crossed by a footbridge. Another approach is from Balerno, instead of Mid Calder, along the old Lanark Road, which at times has quite heavy motor traffic, a walk of five miles, sometimes through avenues of trees, and again in the open, with spacious views southwards of the Pentland range, across either a wooded valley or, as it may be, bare moorland. We shall pass on this road some of the old change-houses of coaching days, "Boll o' Bere", "House of Muir", and as already mentioned, the half-way house of "Little Vantage".

Colzium and Cairns

But having reached by either route the path to the Cauldstane Slap, we notice on the right, Harperrig Reservoir, into which the infant Water of Leith with its tributaries discharges. At the far end of the reservoir are the ruins of Cairns Castle, which in its prime belonged to Sir George Crichton, High Admiral of Scotland, and Earl of Caithness, who charged himself with warding this pass of the Cauldstane Slap through the Pentlands, which in later times became the drove road most commonly frequented by dealers conveying sheep and cattle between the Scots and English markets. In the good old times it was used by freebooters from the south, Scotts, Armstrongs and the rest, who so late as 1600 took eighty cattle, besides horses, southwards with them after wounding and killing those who tried to prevent them. In 1582 the occupants of East Cairns suffered, at the hands of Armstrong and Liddell, the raiding by night of ewes and wedders which lay at Hairhope.

Colzium, which lies further south, together with Cairns and other properties, came into the hands of Michael Linning, W.S., in the early part of the 19th century. He was a subscriber to and Treasurer of the scheme for building the National Monument on the Calton Hill, towards the erection of which he offered in 1830 as much stone as would complete it from a freestone quarry, which he discovered in the West Cairn Hill. He had also a scheme for using the peat on the moor as a fuel, and anticipated some ideas, only realised in recent times, for utilising the Leith's head waters for the Edinburgh water supply, and for supplementing the water power of the various mills. In 1598, Colzium, which had a tower, was raided of cattle by Scott of Branxholm's men, some of the cattle being however returned to the owner. Stevenson, in *Weir of Hermiston*, brings in "the four black brothers of Cauldstone-slap".

Cauldstane Slap

Three miles from the Lanark Road we reach the watershed which separates the moorland scenery of the northern side for the more varied scenery of the south. The "Slap" (meaning "pass") lies between East Cairn Hill (1839 feet) and West Cairn Hill (1844 feet); the cairn on the latter is now a circular grass covered mound of stones 3 feet 6 inches in height. The "Cauldstane Slapp" is shown on a map of 1755 and alongside the name is noted "Road to Queensferry". It must have been this way that James IV travelled in November 1490 when he bought a horse in Linlithgow and rode on it "furth of Lythqow to Lynton before day". Amongst the many references to the Covenanters in the *Register of the Privy Council* it is recorded that the Council had received a report of a conventicle held at "Caldstaineslope" on Sunday, 8th June 1684, attended by some 200 or 300 men and women, the men armed with blunderbusses, swords, and pistols. The heritors were threatened with punishment for permitting the conventicle and General Dalyell was instructed to discover and apprehend those who had been present. J. W. Buchan in his *History of Peeblesshire* quotes a charter of about 1370 which refers to "the high road of the Carnes . . . and along that road on the north side of the Cauldstane". It was in use for centuries as the main drove road for cattle bought at Crieff Tryst, and later Falkirk Tryst, from the northern crofts and farms and driven to the English markets by West Linton and Peebles. In the reverse direction sheep from the Linton market, to the number of some 30,000 annually at the end of the 18th century, were driven north to the Highland grazings.

The path from the summit descends the valley of the Lyne Water to Baddinsgill Reservoir, formed in 1924 to supply water to Bathgate, from which a road goes down to West Linton. The 1755 map shows the road of that time on the east side of the valley from Cairnmuir, and the pedestrian, if so minded, can cross the Lyne Water at a point half a mile below Baddinsgill, and beyond the last plantation, where a signpost "Public footpath to Carlops by Stonypath" points down to a footbridge, and then at the junction beyond Stonypath, either turn right to follow the road over the hill to West Linton or turn left along the Old Biggar Road to Carlops.

Cairnmuir

The house of Cairnmuir occupied a site close to Baddinsgill House, the mansion seen within the trees on the left while descending to the footbridge. The estate of Cairnmuir was bought in the late 15th century by Sir Richard Lawson of Hierigs, provost of Edinburgh in 1492 and again in 1504. (High Riggs and Lady Lawson Street are reminders of the Edinburgh connection). Two of the incidents connected with his family are described by Lindsay of Pitscottie in his *Historie and Cronicles of Scotland.* Sir Richard had a daughter, whose beauty brought two rivals for her hand, William Meldrum of the Binns, whom the lady favoured, and Sir Luke Stirling. Determined to win the lady, Stirling with fifty armed men attacked Meldrum, with only five men, on the way between Edinburgh and Leith. In the unequal contest twentyfive of Stirling's followers were slain or wounded; Meldrum, covered with wounds, was left for dead, but, says Pitscottie, he "lived fiftie years thairaftir". The other incident concerns Sir Richard's son, also Richard of Cairnmuir. On the eve of Flodden a midnight cry was heard at the Cross in Edinburgh, where a strange apparition, "Plotcock", (apparently representing the Devil), summoned all men whom he named to appear before his master within forty days. Richard Lawson heard the cry from his gallery stair opposite the Cross and, getting his purse, threw a crown over the stair calling out "I appeal from that summons judgment and sentence thereof and takes me all whole in the mercy of God and Christ Jesus his son". And, so, it is said, he alone, out of all who had been named in the summons, returned from Flodden.

In the early 18th century young John Lawson of Cairnmuir married Elizabeth Sempill, daughter of the laird of Cathcart, and a descendant of James II, by eloping with her one night when she was on a visit to her grandfather at Lamington House, her parents having chosen another suitor. In 1745 when Lady Cathcart, now a widow, had a visit from some of Prince Charles's highlanders who burst into her room, she first rebuked them for entering her room without uncovering their heads, and then gave them a meal. The Lawson association with Cairnmuir ceased in 1839.

Bridgehouse

Where the modern road from Baddinsgill passes the gate to the golf course, Medwyn House will be seen on the left; it stands on the site of the Bridgehouse or Brighouse Inn, which stood here in coaching days and lost its trade when the new road was built in 1833. An innkeeper at the Brighouse, Thomas Graham, was a friend of Robert Burns, who came twice and not finding his friend at home scratched on a pane "Honest Graham, aye the same, never to be found at hame". The haugh here was the original site of the Linton markets until removed by the Earl of Teviot to a site on the west side of the village, and later transferred to Lanark.

West Linton

Linton (now West Linton to distinguish it from East Linton), was originally known as Linton Roderyck. A church of that name existed in the 12th century, but the present church was built in 1782 and remodelled in 1871. The interior is more beautifully decorated than most country places of worship. A part of the walls and the front of the gallery are covered with carved woodwork, with here and there a text of scripture; this was the work of Miss Fergusson, daughter of Sir William Fergusson of Spitalhaugh, surgeon to Prince Albert, Queen Victoria's consort. The gate posts have heraldic panels, one dated 1601, with the initials IL for James Lawson. In the south east corner of the older part of the churchyard is the burial aisle of the Lawsons of Cairnmuir, and of the Douglases of Garvaldfoot, the latter having a large recumbent slab, carved in relief and with a Latin inscription referring to George and Elizabeth Douglas, with one date 1630, the other uncertain. Some of the grave stones in the churchyard have 17th century dates—1667, 1668 and 1697; one unusual tombstone, which has since disappeared, marked the grave of James Oswald of Spittal, the victim of a shooting accident on Slipperfield Loch in 1726. Oswald, who was of a very sociable and hospitable disposition, possessed a hall table of marble, on which his festivities were conducted. This table was used as his tombstone, with the following inscription, as here translated:—

"This marble table, sitting at which I have often cultivated good living (propitiated my tutelar genius), I have desired to be placed over me when dead. Stop, traveller, whoever thou art; here thou mayst recline, and, if the means are at hand, mayst enjoy this table as I formerly did. If thou doest so in the right and proper way, thou wilt neither desecrate this monument nor offend my manes. Nov. 28th, 1726. Farewell."

Laird Gifford

The houses in the village, as far as order and arrangement are concerned, might have dropped from the clouds. In the centre stands the Clock Tower, built over the old village well, with a puffy-faced stone effigy of Lady Gifford. James Gifford, usually called Laird Gifford, who was a stonemason and sculptor in the middle of the 17th century, erected in the village in 1666, a statue of his wife and his four children, with their figures placed around his wife, one at each corner of the pedestal. Before the work was finished he became the father of a fifth child, and the only place he could find for the additional sculpture was on the mother's head. The figures of the children gradually fell off, and only the figure of Lady Gifford has survived. A more interesting example of Gifford's work is the panel built into the wall of Gifford's Stone House, a modern dwelling on the site of his original house, opposite the Raemartin Hotel. In the central panel are the figures of Gifford and his wife (Iames Gifferd : Ewpham Veatch). The panel on the right again shows Gifford and his wife (IG : EV). The panel on the left is divided into four smaller panels, in each of them two figures; between the upper and lower panels are carved the words: "Six progenetors of Iames Gifferd wi(th) his awne portract and eldest sone". In the panels are six figures representing the Giffords from 1445 onwards; in the bottom right hand panel is Gifford himself holding a hawk on his wrist, and his eldest son holding a rose. The inscription at the foot, now much weathered and incomplete, was recorded when in better condition as reading "Wrought by me Iames Geferd Architector ye 7th May 1660."

12. Route 12a—Crosswood (West Calder) to Dolphinton or Dunsyre 13 Miles

Roman Camp—Crosswood—Henshaw Hill—Covenanter's Grave —Dolphinton.

FROM West Calder to Dolphinton is a full thirteen miles and to West Linton the best part of fourteen, either way a fine long tramp over bracing moors where only an occasional wayfarer finds his way. (A lift to Crosswood on the A70 cuts off four miles). These distant routes over the Pentlands are so little frequented that although they are rights of way they can seldom be described as paths. There is in parts a faintly discernible track, but mostly the pedestrian has to rely on the map and on his sense of direction, preferably with the aid of a compass in case of mist. But these wide and unfrequented moors are to many even more attractive than the better known paths nearer Edinburgh. One of the hindrances to using these routes is the distance from public transport on the north side of the hills, but even if an extra four miles of road is added by starting from West Calder, which has a good bus service from Edinburgh, the walk over the hills to Dolphinton or Dunsyre or even West Linton is easily within the compass of a long summer afternoon, and there is an excellent bus service to take one home from Dolphinton.

CROSSWOOD

The road from West Calder (B7008) turns southwards and reaches its highest point on Camilty Hill on which, just south of the summit, there is clearly distinguished on the left the ramparts of the Roman Camp of Castle Greg. It is a small camp, never completely excavated, but its rectangular form, fragments of glass and pottery, and a find last century of Roman coins in the vicinity are sufficient to confirm its Roman origin. Past the camp the road descends to the Lang Whang, where a quarter of a mile along to the right is the service road to Crosswood Reservoir, with a post indicating that it leads to the public path to Dunsyre. Follow this road until you come to a wood on the right, where a sign marks the right of way along the edge of the field. At the far end of the trees stop before crossing the stile to trace out the route ahead for, it must be understood, the words "public path" are a legalistic term and not something you will necessarily find on the ground. From the stile the route does not go to the farm steading seen ahead, but goes half left across the field to another stile at its south-east corner. Look beyond this stile and you will see a post about half-way up the slope ahead, somewhat to the left of a cart track ascending the hill and well to the left of the trees on the top of this nearer hill. Beyond this post you should see on the distant hill two trees, with a smaller third, and a post on the sky-line to their right marking the right of way. If you now cross the field from the first stile, you will find a second stile at a gate across a cart road. Follow this road to a third stile beside another gate with a post just a few yards beyond it. Now go uphill to the left of the cart track, up by the post on the slope. Now bear slightly to the right past another post and as you progress in this direction you will gradually approach a stone dike on the right. Turn left along the near side of the dike until, about a mile from Mid Crosswood, there is a stile and a gate. Cross here and, negotiating the Small Burn, continue in the same direction as before (S.S.E.), gradually moving away from the dike, and aiming for a dip ahead on Henshaw Hill where the route is marked by a post. (Up the burn, 100 yards S.W. from the stile, is the Hunters' Well).

Henshaw Hill

Splendid views are a feature of Pentland walks, and from Henshaw Hill, as from many others, the view northwards over West Lothian embraces the Ochils and a long line of Highland hills from Ben Lomond to the crowded peaks of Perthshire. On crossing the shoulder of Henshaw Hill a gate is seen ahead on the right and beyond it a signpost pointing in three directions: to Harburn; to Dunsyre and West Linton; to Auchengray. (Harburn, near Crosswood, had once a railway station). For the route from Auchengray coming in at this post see Route 12b.

For Dolphinton or Dunsyre continue south-east, first descending to a ford over the Garval Syke, the headwaters of the Medwin, which in time will reach the Clyde; the post marking the line is seen ahead (S.S.E.) on the col between White Craig and Darlees Rig. A stiff climb up some 400 feet is rewarded at the top by an extensive view to the south. Once over the ridge be careful not to descend into the valley on the right where you see a small reservoir and the waterworks road; keep along the high ground on your left to Black Law, where the Covenanter's Grave is a little below the summit on the south-west side.

Covenanter's Grave

The stone marking the Covenanter's Grave stands some three feet high and bears the following inscription: "Sacred to the memory of a Covenanter, who fought and was wounded at Rullion Green, November 28th 1666, and who died at Oaken Bush the day after the battle, and was buried here by Adam Sanderson of Blackhill". This

Covenanter, badly wounded, was struggling homewards to Ayrshire. He had called at the farmhouse of Blackhill, (now a ruined cottage above Medwynhead), and wounded as he was he could not be dissuaded from pressing on. The farmer, Adam Sanderson, gave what help he could, but the fugitive's strength soon failed him. About a mile from Blackhill he died and was buried by the farmer.

In 1817 Blackwood's Magazine reported that the story of the Covenanter was still known in the Sanderson family, who for generations had been shepherds in the place, and in that year its truth had been confirmed by digging at the spot marked by a rude stone. The remains of a skeleton and fragments of clothes with leather buttons were found, and were reburied. Some years later the present memorial stone was erected.

These moors were the centre of Covenanting gatherings. In the remote glen of the Medwin to the east of Black Law is Roger's Kirk, a rock where conventicles were held. The Rev. Donald Cargill preached his last sermon on the common of Dunsyre; William Veitch of Westhills, and Learmonth, the Laird of Newholm, leaders at Rullion Green, were from this quarter. A field meeting was held on the first day of June 1684, at the Cairn Hill, and again seven days later at "Caldstaineslope or some other place thereabout", to the number of three hundred men and women. The "pulpit rock" behind the West Cairn Hill was traditionally said to have been the rostrum from which the audience was addressed.

From the Covenanter's Grave continue south-east down the ridge to the waterworks road at a sign post: Crosswood; Dolphinton. For the route along this road to West Linton see Route 13; although the road is not the old right of way (see below), it provides an easier and quicker route to West Linton. For Dunsyre or Dolphinton cross the road and continue south across the moor for less than half a mile to another sign post which is on the line of the old east-west right of way and points in four directions: Crosswood; Boston Cottage; Dolphinton; West Linton. From this sign post make south for the cone shaped hill rising beyond a plantation of fir trees on the far edge of the moor. Shortly a post (no sign) will be seen slightly to the left, then a second and a third post. Here the routes diverge. For Dolphinton bear to the left and keep along the east bank of the West Water until the farm buildings at Garvald come in sight beyond the Medwin Water, here crossed by a footbridge. Go through the farm steading to the road leading in a mile and a quarter to the Biggar road, half a mile from Dolphinton.

Dolphinton

For 70 years this point was the terminus of two separate railways.

The Linton and Dolphinton Railway, opened in July 1864 and absorbed in the North British Railway in July 1865, ran from Leadburn Junction on the Peebles railway via stations at Lamancha, Macbiehill (for Carlops), and Broomlee (for West Linton), to the station at Dolphinton on the east side of the main road. The Carstairs and Dolphinton branch of the Caledonian Railway opened in March 1867, ran from Carstairs via Dunsyre to a station on the west side of the main road; the track of this railway can be seen where it runs parallel to the road from Garvald. The former line became part in due course of the L.N.E.R. system; the latter of the L.M.S. system. These lines were closed down before the last war, but small parts of the two stations can still be seen.

If Dunsyre is the objective and not Dolphinton, from the point (above) where the routes diverge on the moor, continue straight down to the West Water, here crossed by a cart track which can be seen rising beyond the stream and making for the west end of a plantation. Crossing the West Water (no footbridge) presents no difficulty unless after heavy rain. From the plantation the cart track goes down to Easton Farm, whence a road goes to Dunsyre.

Taking the route to Crosswood from south to north, the signposts at Garvald Farm and beyond make the route clear. If Dunsyre is the start, at Easton Farm go left round the south side of the first of the farm buildings to get on to the cart track which goes over the hill by the west end of the plantation.

Route 12b—Auchengray to Dolphinston or Dunsyre
11 miles

THIS is a different starting point from Route 12a, but joins that route on Henshaw Hill, and thereafter, from the Garval Syke and by the Covenanter's Grave, is the same. Starting from Auchengray go about a quarter mile north of the village to a road which branches right by Easterhouse, skirting Tarbrax, and in three miles joins the Lang Whang close to its highest point. Here a signpost on the east side of the A70 points to West Linton. It is close to a gate; at this gate look east, along the north side of a fence, and in the distance is seen Henshaw Hill, the first objective. On the near ridge, a post, somewhat left of the fence, marks the line. From this post the route follows the curve of the Dry Burn, which is below on the right, and gradually ascends the southern slope of Henshaw Hill. Once the crest of the slope is reached a signpost will be seen ahead, to the right of a gate in a stone dike; this is the post described in Route 12a, and you will turn right here to follow that route over the hill and past the Covenanter's Grave to Dolphinton or Dunsyre.

13. Route 13—Auchengray and Boston Cottage to West Linton or Dolphinton — 13 Miles

Boston Cottage—Left Law—Green Side—Medwynhead—Dry Burn—North Slipperfield—West Linton.

FOR the most distant of the routes over the Pentlands, that by Boston Cottage to West Linton, Auchengray is the nearest starting point with public transport (infrequent). From the village follow the road south for a mile and then turn to the left uphill by the road to the farms of King's Inn and East Yardhouses. A grassy cart track continues the route over the hill, across the North Medwin, and up to the A70 some four miles from Carnwath at Boston Cottage, an inn in old coaching days, but represented now merely by a small grass covered heap of stones on the west side of the road opposite Lingy Knowe. The name is no longer shown on the O.S. map. but it is retained on several of the Scottish Rights of Way signposts for direction purposes.

LEFT LAW

On the roadside opposite "Boston Cottage" a signpost (Public footpath to Dunsyre 5 and West Linton 9) marks the start of a broad track going up through a gap in the plantation on Lingy Knowe. Beyond the plantation the track can be clearly seen going across the moor. After crossing the Westruther Burn it climbs to the slight dip between Horse Law and Left Law and goes up the slope of Left Law to a gate. Beyond this gate is a signpost, about two miles from the A70, with three signs: Boston Cottage; Dunsyre; West Linton. It is one of the advantages of this walk that in bad weather it can be shortened by turning down this path to Dunsyre (see Route 14), or two miles farther on branching off down by the West Water to Garvald and Dolphinton.

At the signpost on the southern slope of Left Law you quit the good path and for West Linton strike due east to a post seen on the next ridge; there is no real track to it. From this post you see another post farther east, an old wooden sign, barely decipherable, "Drove Road to West Linton by Medwynhead". Few traces of a drove road remain and your guide must be the posts or compass. From this signpost you look straight ahead to the broad pass between Bleak Law and Mid Hill and you may just discern a post on the sky-line low down on the south slope of Bleak Law, at Green Side, a little above the level of the pass. To reach it go round in a slight curve to the left, so as to avoid the wetter ground, and aim for the middle of Bleak Law, where there is a post and a gate in the fence on its near slope. Once past the gate go to the right round the slope of Bleak Law, keeping a high level, and you will reach the post already seen and find it well above the level of the pass.

Green Side

Ahead is a wide view with the Mendick Hill prominent. To the left of it, a mile and a half distant, are the trees at Medwynhead on the line of the drove road and right of way. The route to it is indicated by a post ahead and below in the midst of the heather, but because the ground there is rather boggy keep more to the left along the eastern flank of Bleak Law. (In misty weather take care not to go down by the middle of the pass and the small burn which runs through Easton Farm unless you wish to take a short cut to Dunsyre.) Nearing the gully of the West Water you see a post short of the stream—the crossing is easier more to the left—and another signpost on the moor beyond the stream. This signpost is the one described in Route 12a with the four signs—Crosswood, Boston Cottage, Dolphinton, West Linton—where the drove road is crossed by the right of way from Crosswood and where you can branch right to Dolphinton or Dunsyre. From the same post the Covenanter's Grave is less than a mile north near the summit of Black Law.

Medwynhead

For West Linton there are two alternatives from this signpost. (a) You can continue east on the right of way, aiming rather to the left of the next post which you see on Cairn Knowe, so that you have an easier gradient beyond it down to the Medwin Water and Medwynhead, a lonely habitation which is half way in distance between Boston Cottage and West Linton, although much the easier half is to come. Crossing the Medwin Water could be difficult after rain; there is no longer a footbridge. A little upstream will be seen the ruin of Blackhill, where the wounded Covenanter called (see Route 12a). The right of way passes in front of Medwynhead and goes up the approach road through some trees; immediately beyond them the road bends right (and goes down to Ferniehaugh and Garvald), whilst the right of way to West Linton branches to the left. There are no visible signs here of the right of way or of the old drove road which went east across the moor to the north side of the Dry Burn, although it is said to have been in use at the turn of the century. As the going is so rough the best plan is to turn uphill to the waterworks road and follow it eastward. You soon quit the watershed of the Clyde and descend into the watershed of the Tweed. The road keeps along the left of the Dry Burn and at North Slipperfield joins the surfaced road which goes to West Linton. A little before North Slipperfield the road runs high above the valley on the right; the right of way at this point is lower down, where it is joined by the track on the right (Route 14) coming from Dunsyre and Ferniehaugh. The two miles from the junction of the tracks at Slipperfield Mount to West Linton are on an easy gradient down through the golf course to the Old Biggar Road, with a final half mile down the Baddinsgill Road to the village.

(b) The alternative from the four-finger signpost at the "crossways" is to turn north here towards Black Law and in less than half a mile join the waterworks roads and follow it east to North Slipperfield as described above. This alternative is recommended after rain when crossing the Medwin Water at Medwynhead could be difficult.

Stonypath

As Boston Cottage is difficult to reach if you are dependant on public transport, an alternative is to start from the Stonypath road which leaves the public road (bus service), a mile west of Dunsyre village. The distance by this alternative is shorter by less than a mile. Beyond Stonypath a broad cart track goes north-west up over the moor (keep left at what might be considered a fork), and in a mile and a quarter from the public road the signpost with three signs: Boston Cottage; Dunsyre; West Linton; is reached. There you join the path from Boston Cottage and now turn east to follow the right of way and old drove road as described above.

14. Route 14—Boston Cottage to West Linton via Dunsyre 15 Miles

---

Boston Cottage—Stonypath—Dunsyre—Medwynbank—Ferniehaugh—Nether Cairn—Rumbling Well—North Slipperfield—West Linton.

Boston Cottage to Dunsyre is the easiest crossing of the Pentlands, rising less than 300 feet starting from the Lanark road, and the shortest, only four miles, with another three miles added if starting from Auchengray. Three of the four miles are on a good path; the fourth mile is along the road. The route is the same as Route 13 to the signpost on Left Law, where the path turns downhill to Stonypath and to the main road (bus route) at Anston Burn, just over a mile from the signpost and a mile west of Dunsyre.

In Dunsyre village, just before the old railway embankment, a road branches left to Easton and Medwynbank. In a mile, instead of turning off to Easton, continue ahead by a farm road which crosses the West Water and the Medwin Water, both with footbridges, to Ferniehaugh. Just beyond the West Water a footbridge down on the right is on Route 12 to Garvald and Dolphinton.

At Ferniehaugh, at the point where the road bends back to Garvald, a gate on the left is the start of the right of way, here a cart track along the edge of a field, to West Linton.

Nether Cairn

Half a mile north-east of Ferniehaugh and 150 yards on the left of the path, is a massive circular cairn, the "Nether Cairn", 50 feet in diameter and 12 feet in height. In the *Inventory of Ancient Monuments in Peeblesshire* it is described as the best preserved example of its kind in the country and appears to be virtually untouched. There are slight indications of a surrounding ditch, some 6 feet in width, about 3 feet from the cairn. Half a mile farther along the path is a second cairn on the left, the "Upper Cairn", fully 70 feet in diameter and still standing to a height of 14 feet, although many of the stones have been carted away. The path, which has been running high above the hollow down which flows the Garvald Burn, now descends to its level; here, half way down the slope on the right, is the "Rumbling Well", where the burn gushes out from the ground. In another mile the path joins the waterworks road (Route 13) at North Slipperfield, a mile and a half from West Linton.

15. Route 15—Along the Hill Tops 8 Miles

West Kip—East Kip—Scald Law—Carnethy—Turnhouse Hill—Castlelaw—Allermuir—Caerketton.

THE eastern half of the Pentlands include the highest and finest of the hills; Turnhouse Hill, Carnethy, Scald Law, East Kip and West Kip form a steep and narrow range providing fine views and good walking, with a distinct path all the way. Whether we start from the south-western end of this range so as to have the sun, and for most of the year, also the wind behind us, or from the northern end, this ridge walk can begin and end on the Biggar road or be extended into a cross country walk between Balerno and Flotterstone.

If starting from the far end of this range the col between Cap Law and West Kip is the point to aim for; the shortest approach is by the Eastside Farm access road (no vehicles), which leaves the Biggar Road half a mile beyond Silverburn and has the signpost "Footpath to Balerno". Other approaches are by one of the two paths going uphill from Nine Mile Burn, or from Balerno by Bavelaw and the path to Nine Mile Burn.

West Kip and Scald Law

The climb from the col up West Kip (1806 feet) is steep but short; on its rocky crest we find that it forms a ridge rather than a peak. The view is very good; behind appear the Pentlands stretching into the distance in range after range; in front is Scald Law rising steeply from Loganlee Reservoir, with Allermuir and Caerketton providing a more distant background. East Kip (1750 feet) is lower and less outstanding than West Kip. Scald Law (1899 feet), the next to be climbed, is not only the highest of the Pentland Hills, but is also very much larger in bulk than the Kips and the top is more of a plateau than a peak. By reason of its height Scald Law provides a more extensive view than its neighbours, except where its spur, South Black Hill, curtails the view to the south.

Carnethy and Turnhouse

From Scald Law there is a good drop to the Kirk Road, the pass from Loganlee to the Penicuik road, and then another climb to Carnethy Hill (1830 feet), which has on its summit a Bronze Age Cairn. The ridge then narrows to Turnhouse Hill (1636 feet), bounded on the north side by Glencorse Reservoir. There is no way down by the reservoir; one must go to the right over a spur with some trees on it, and then down the side of a dike close to the Glencorse Burn until the footbridge over the burn is reached near Flotterstone. In the reverse direction starting from Flotterstone, follow the glen road to the first gate on the left, where a track leads to a footbridge over Glencorse Burn. From here there is a distinct path up Turnhouse Hill.

Allermuir and Caerketton

From Flotterstone the hill walk can be continued to Hillend on days when the firing range is not in use by the army. First, go along the main road to Crosshouse Farm and then uphill to Castlelaw Fort, from which a broad track goes up the east slope of Castlelaw.

From Castlelaw Hill one gets what is probably the finest view in the Pentlands; deep below is the full length of Glencorse Reservoir curving round the base of Turnhouse, with the long valley stretching up to Loganlee Reservoir, and the fine ridge of hills, Turnhouse, Carnethy, Scald Law and the distant pyramid of West Kip.

Returning to the path, we follow it over Fala Knowe, and leave it again when it crosses a dike, so that we can go straight uphill to the top of Allermuir (1619 feet), where in clear weather the view extends from the Cheviot to the Grampians, with Edinburgh and the Forth laid out below like a map. The path continues over the top of Caerketton and descends through Hillend Park to Lothianburn.

16. Route 16—The Old Biggar Road : The Roman Road

(a) The Old Biggar Road

THE old Biggar Road, which was the highway until the present road was constructed in 1833, has seen centuries of Scottish history from the time of the Romans who came this way.

ASSOCIATIONS OF THE BIGGAR ROAD

If the historical or literary associations be uppermost, then one recalls how Christopher North escaped from Edinburgh on the Dumfries coach, which came this way as far as West Linton, and was bowled along to his favourite pools on the Tweed, near the Crook Inn; and how Thomas Carlyle journeyed to and fro by Erickstane and the Devil's Beef Tub to or from Ecclefechan. How he hated the journey! Woodhouselee recalls the Tytlers and early visits from Walter Scott after he started housekeeping near Lasswade. We have time to think of the battle of Rullion Green on the hillside to our right while climbing upwards out of Glencorse Glen, where General Thomas Dalziel defeated 900 westland Covenanters on 28th November 1666 (Route 2). The father of George Meikle Kemp, architect of the Scott Monument, was a shephered at Nine- Mile-Burn. There are associations with Allan Ramsay at Newhall, and his *Gentle Shepherd* has lent undying lustre to Habbie's Howe, which we pass on entering Carlops. Dr. John Brown wrote *Rab and His Friends* as a lecture for his native Biggar, and felt that he read it but badly; when published the Doctor found sympathetic friends all over the world. And never had a father's memory a finer tribute than that which he wrote, "done to the quick", in his well-known Letter to John Cairns, D.D. And Biggar has associations with William Ewart Gladstone, whose great-great-grandfather came to live here in 1679; the names of several of the family are recorded on tombstones in Biggar Churchyard.

A PILGRIM ROAD

At an earlier date this was the road followed by pilgrims going from Edinburgh to the shrine of St. Ninian at Whithorn. King James IV made frequent pilgrimages, and the royal accounts show several payments during his reign (1488–1513) to the "wife" in Biggar, where he usually spent the first night of the journey when riding. In 1507 after the Queen's serious illness he made the pilgrimage on foot and the accounts record payments "to the wife of the Mure (House of Muir) alehouse", 7s for breakfast; in Linton 14s for dinner; reaching Dolphinton that night where he gave the priest 18s for fire, candle and food. Next day he reached Biggar for dinner. James also travelled this road on sporting outings; in September 1505 he had dinner in Dunsyre "at hawking".

The modern road to Biggar and the old road diverge about a mile north of Silverburn and there is no great difficulty in following the track of the old road, on the right of the present road, from Silverburn to Nine Mile Burn. For the next mile the old road is still in use and then it becomes a footpath, ending in a short descent to the main road. On the south side of Carlops, at Hartside, the old road strikes off to the right, first a grassy track and then from Linton Muir a farm road until it joins at Stonypath corner the surfaced road which descends to the bridge over the Lyne Water.

In the *New Statistical Account* of 1834 the parish minister of Linton reports that the old road from Edinburgh was ill-directed, the approaches to the village of Linton from east and west being extremely difficult for carriages, but the new road had been opened in 1833, and two new inns had been built on it at Linton and Rutherford with post horses and every accommodation. From the Lyne Water the old road went up by the present Medwin House, where once stood the "Brighouse" Inn; nowadays you go straight uphill from the bridge to the Baddinsgill road, then turn left to rejoin the old road at the entrance to the golf course.

The old road onward is marked by a signpost where it leaves the modern road through the golf course. Just past the fork, on the left, are the remains of an old inn, and beyond it the road crosses the West Water by a single arch bridge on which a panel is inscribed "Erected 1620. Restored 1899". The old road continues as a farm road in almost a straight line for the next two miles (see the next chapter for traces of the Roman road), and then beyond Ingraston Farm goes round Sandy Hill to join the modern road close to the Garvald road junction half a mile north of Dolphinton village. Between Dolphinton and Biggar old and new roads coincide except for the short stretch north of Candyburn.

(*b*) *The Roman Road*

In A.D.80 the Roman legions, under the command of Agricola, then governor of Britain, invaded Scotland, and, with interruptions, and under successive commanders, continued in occupation of southern Scotland for over a century. During that time they constructed several roads, the two roads from the south being Dere Street from York to Inveresk by Lauderdale and the western route from Carlisle by Annandale into Clydesdale. From the upper Clyde the Roman road to Inveresk and the Forth runs along the south-eastern edge of the Pentlands. A stretch of it is visible three miles north of Biggar and parts of it can be seen in several places north of Dolphinton.

About a quarter mile along the Old Biggar Road from the Garvald Road at Dolphinton are the sand quarries on Sandy Hill. On the east side of this hill, just above the edge of a field, is a broad shelf representing the Roman Road; this can be seen looking north from the Garvald road junction. Just north of this in the next field is a prominent embankment, 65 yards long, on a line, through the trees, with the point over a mile ahead where the old road and the Roman road pass the end of a plantation. Little is visible on the ground in the next four fields, but at three quarters of a mile beyond Ingraston, where the Old Biggar Road has made a bend to the right to the "Springs", the mound of the Roman road is quite distinct only 20 yards to the right, and can be traced both back and ahead. At the next plantation it is less than 10 yards from the old road, a well preserved mound six paces wide. A short length is next visible along the east side of Hardgatehead Cottage, and it is quite distinct in the next plantation, on the right of the old road. In the next field short stretches of causeway remain but are not readily noticed; and in the plantation by South Slipperfield Cottage it is overgrown.

Nothing of the Roman road is seen for another two miles. At the point beyond the Lyne Water where the road turns left to Stonypath, the Roman road diverges from the old Biggar road, until at the plantation at the top of the second field it is about 60 yards from the old road. There is little to be seen here but beyond the plantation the shelf of the Roman road can be seen from the old road, about 90 yards up on the left and running parallel for over half a mile. It can be seen up a short road opposite Fairslacks Farm, where the causeway crosses a gully, and continues north for another 200 yards when broken ground has left no trace.

The medieval road passes Linton Muir (formerly Waterloo) and in another third of a mile bends to the right. At this point, immediately on the left, a cutting, rather obscured and blocked, points north to the western side of the wood at Carlops. This is the Roman road; to reach the continuation of it go down the hollow-way on the left. This leads to a causeway across the saddle and up the next slope to the west side of a wall, where it becomes a shelf, and by the west side of the plantation to the Carlops Burn. Beyond this the line of the Roman road is uncertain; today the modern road can be reached by a passage along the south side of the burn.

North of Carlops no certain traces of the Roman road are to be found until beyond Nine Mile Burn. Here the Old Biggar Road may be on the line of the Roman Road as, a little over half a mile ahead, the Roman Road can be seen again on the ridge above a quarry. It is in good preservation for 500 yards, with quarry pits on either side. North of this point it aimed for the Roman station at Inveresk but no trace of it has been found.

NOTE: The Roman Road is described in detail in J. K. St. Joseph, *The Roman Occupation of S.W. Scotland* (ed. by S. N. Miller), published in 1952.

17. Circular Walks

THE following is a selection of circular walks for those who wish to return to the starting point; others can be planned from the Pentland Hills map.

1. From Slateford go up Craiglockhart Dell and Colinton Dell; return by the old railway "Walkway" (Routes 3 b and c).

2. From Hunter's Tryst, near Fairmilehead, to Swanston, then ascend by the burnside to the summit of Allermuir (1617 feet). Continue over the hill and down its west slope into Howden Glen, and go down this glen to Dreghorn Mains and Hunter's Tryst. (Routes 1 and 5). (Not to be undertaken when the rifle range at the foot of Howden Glen is in use.)

3. From Colinton go up Dreghorn Loan to Howden Glen and continue by the track to the west of Allermuir over to Castlelaw and Flotterstone. Return to Colinton by Glencorse Reservoir and Bonaly Reservoir. (Routes 5 and 6). (See note to (2) above.)

4. From Colinton go up Dreghorn Loan to the trees at the foot of Howden Glen, then uphill to the right until Bonaly Reservoir is reached. Descend by Bonaly Public Park to Colinton. (Routes 5 and 6). (See note to (2) above.)

5. From Colinton go along Woodhall Road and down West Mills Road; then follow the valley "Walkway" up the Water of Leith to Balerno. Return by Malleny House, Lymphoy, Blinkbonny and Woodhall House to Colinton. This can be shortened by turning at Currie. (Routes 4 b and c).

6. From Colinton ascend by Fernielaw Avenue to Torduff Reservoir, then follow the waterworks road past Clubbiedean Reservoir to East Kinleith. Descend by Kinleith Burn (the Poet's Glen) to the Water of Leith and return by the "Walkway" to Colinton. (Routes 4d and b).

7. From Colinton ascend Bonaly Road to Bonaly Reservoir; beyond it bear right and go down the valley until the Currie path comes in on the right. Turn up the Currie path, through the Maiden's Cleuch, and descend to the "Crossroads" at Kinleith. Here turn right to reach Colinton either by Clubbiedean and Torduff Reservoirs, or by the direct route along the north slope of Torphin Hill. (Routes 6, 7 and 4d).

8. From Currie Bridge ascend the Kirkgate to "Crossroads"; turn right to Harlaw Farm and go left here to reach Harlaw Reservoir. Follow the path alongside this reservoir and Threipmuir to the Bavelaw Road and descend to Balerno. Return to Currie either by

the valley "Walkway" or by Malleny House and Lymphoy. (Routes 7, 8 and 4).

9. From (Balerno) Harlaw Farm go by the path alongside the reservoirs to the Bavelaw road. Ascend the hill to Bavelaw Castle and go through the Green Cleuch to Loganlee Reservoir, then down by Glencorse Reservoir to the signpost pointing the way to Currie and Balerno. Where the path forks after the Maiden's Cleuch keep to the left fork for Harlaw. (Routes 8 and 7).

10. From Marchbank, above Balerno, go uphill by the avenue to Bavelaw and then follow the path to Nine Mile Burn. Here go along the old road from Habbie's Howe Hotel for a quarter mile and turn uphill by Spittal Farm to cross to the North Esk Reservoir. Turn north by the reservoir to the Bore Stane; descend on the north side to Listonshiels and here turn right by first a track and then a road to Marchbank. (Routes 9 and 10).

11. From Silverburn on the Biggar Road go south to the farm road (signpost "To Balerno") for Eastside. Continue over the range by the col west of West Kip and descend until past the Logan Burn. Then turn right down the valley of this burn to the head of Loganlee Reservoir, where the "Kirk Road" goes uphill and across the hill to the Biggar Road, a little north of Silverburn. (Routes 9 and 8).

12. From Carlops ascend by the path up the River Esk to the reservoir, then turn right uphill and over the hill to Spittal Farm, and return by the Old Biggar Road to Carlops. (Route 10).

13. From West Linton Golf Course follow the road through the golf course to North Slipperfield, then branch left at the first signpost and again left at the second post. Continue by the path past the Rumbling Well to Ferniehaugh and by road past Garvald House to the Old Biggar Road, returning by Ingraston to West Linton Golf Course. (Routes 14 and 16).

14. From West Linton to North Slipperfield as (13). Then go along the left branch of the waterworks road for 3 miles to the post beyond the Medwin Water, and ascend to the Covenanter's Grave. Return to the post and continue south by Route 12 to the cart road leading left to Medwynbank; then back to North Slipperfield by Ferniehaugh and the Rumbling Well. (Routes 13, 12 and 14).

15. From Dunsyre follow the road to Stonypath and continue by the track to the signpost where Route 13 from Boston Cottage to West Linton is joined. Follow this Route east by Greenside and the West Water to Easton Farm and then back to Dunsyre. (Routes 14 and 13).

18. Round the Pentlands by Cycle or Car

Balerno—The Lang Whang—Carnwath—Dunsyre—West Linton.

FROM Edinburgh round the Pentlands by road is a run of 50 miles, or over 60 if side trips are made by the roads into the hills at Balerno and West Linton. As far as Balerno the places of interest along the Water of Leith and the foot of the Pentlands have been described in earlier routes, and all that need detract the traveller's attention from the road is the splendid view of the hills across the valley of the Water of Leith. Although the city stops at Juniper Green it is not until Balerno that the road escapes from the houses and gets really out into the open.

To make the side trip from Balerno to the hills the road up by the village has to be followed. Beyond the village it rises gently over the moor and stops at Threipmuir Reservoir beside the old ruined farm-house of Redford. The return to the A70 can be made by the same road; or by turning left (west) at Marchbank and following the road round by East Rigg and Cockburnhill, then left at the next fork and past Haughhead Farm, the A70 is reached two miles west of Balerno.

Just before Balerno the main road forks right and ascends Ravelrig Hill, where paths go off on the right by Hannahfield Quarry to Dalmahoy Hill and Kaimes Hill, both crowned by early fortifications and hut circles indicating that they were hill settlements more than two thousand years ago. This road was in stage coach times the road to Lanark, and there still clings to it the atmosphere of its palmy days. At the foot of Kaimes Hill there is on the roadside a farm by the name of Boll of Bere, part of which was once an inn, and out beyond it on the left of the road are House o' Muir and the ruins of Little Vantage, both inns or alehouses in their day. An old toll-house stands near Little Vantage at the start of the path over the Cauldstane Slap. Before a traveller in the age of tolls had got so far he passed and paid at the toll bars at Tynecastle and Ravelrig; truly an expensive outing. Small wonder that one writer complained that towns were "literally hemmed in like a fortified city" by toll-houses.

THE LANG WHANG

Soon Harperrig Reservoir comes into sight and at its far end are seen the ruins of Cairns Castle, built in the 15th century by George Crichton, Admiral of Scotland. Crichton was high in the favour of James II and was created Earl of Caithness, but the title reverted to the King. The lands of Cairns were sold by the Crichtons in the 16th century, and thereafter changed hands frequently. The owner in

1823, Dr. Laird, granted a feu of ground "on the Edinburgh and Lanark Road for the erection thereon of a new Inn and offices to be called the Cairns Castle Inn". The inn later became the school of Causewayend, the hamlet at the road fork near Cairns Castle. In various parts of Scotland the names Causewayend and Causewayhead indicate the site of old stone causeways laid over marshy ground, being maintained in some cases by tolls long before proper roads were made. Beyond Causewayend is the bleakest stretch of the Lanark Road, known to many a weary walker as the "Lang Whang". At the fifteenth milestone is the Halfway House, once another inn where the traveller could rest with the consciousness of half his journey over. Little more than a mile farther west, where afforestation is altering the landscape, a road on the right goes to West Calder. Half a mile along this road can be seen on the right, just south of the Ordnance Survey pillar on Camilty Hill, the outlines of the Roman camp of Castle Greg, a rectangular camp measuring 180 feet by 152 feet, surrounded by ramparts still of considerable height. The bleak main road continues to rise to 1098 feet near the nineteenth milestone and the road which forks right to Auchengray. The valley of the Forth is left behind, for the burns now crossed on the descent to Carnwath make their way to the Clyde.

Carnwath

At the end of the hills and at the junction of the roads north and south of the Pentlands stands the old village of Carnwath with several old inns to indicate its former importance as a stage on the road to Ayr. The village centres round the old 16th century Cross on which is given a list, added at a later date, of the distances on the roads from Edinburgh to Ayr and Glasgow to Peebles. In St. Mary's Aisle, a fragment of the north transept of a church built in 1424, lie many of the Somervilles, lords of Carnwath from the 12th to the 17th centuries. Little remains of their stronghold, Couthalley Castle, on the north of Carnwath; its story and the history of the family will be found in *The Baronial House of Somerville*, by James Somerville. More ancient than any of the buildings in the village is the Mote or early fort to the west of the village from which the place is supposed to take its name.

From Carnwath the road to Edinburgh by the south of the hills goes to Newbigging, a village with another fine Cross bearing the date 1693, but possibly much older. Here there is a choice of two roads to Dolphinton, the left one being taken for preference as it keeps nearer to the hills, and passes through the village of Dunsyre, which has an old church where iron jougs will be seen affixed to the wall.

Dunsyre

Cyclists can quit the main road at Dunsyre, turning left just before the old railway embankment, and cycle most of the way by Medwynbank and North Slipperfield, a pleasant route to West Linton. On the south-east of Dunsyre, where the road crosses the South Medwin, is Newholm, belonging to the ancient family of the Lockharts of Lee and Carnwath, associated with the famous "Lee Penny", which provided Sir Walter Scott with a principal incident in his novel *The Talisman*. Sir Simon Lockhart of Lee and Carnwath was one of the band of Scottish Knights under Sir James Douglas conveying the heart of Robert Bruce to the Holy Land. It is said that in a battle with the Saracens, Sir Simon made prisoner a wealthy Emir, for whom a ransom was paid, and in this ransom was included a small triangular stone of unknown origin, dull red in colour, which has been set in a piece of silver coin. Water in which this talisman is dipped is believed to have unusual curative properties. Keeping to the main road from Dunsyre will bring the traveller to the Biggar-Edinburgh road at Dolphinton, which has one of the smallest parish churches in Scotland. The prominent monument on Kippit Hill (opposite the road to Garvald House) is to Captain Kenneth Mackenzie of Dolphinton, killed in the war of 1914–18. Sir Archibald Geikie in his book on *The Scenery of Scotland* refers to this hill and its supposed association with Michael Scott, the wizard: "There is a deep gash through a sandy ridge at the south end of the Pentland Hills, and not far off stands a green conical sand-hill. The wizard is said to have dug the trench and piled up the hill in the course of a single night." The two railways which once had stations here are described in an earlier chapter.

West Linton

A pleasant side trip from West Linton on a good motoring road is to Baddinsgill, 3 miles up in the Pentlands, where the large reservoir, finished in 1924 for Bathgate water supply, fills the valley. From West Linton (described under Route 11), the main road goes on to Carlops, passing on the right the house of Rutherford, where an inn was built when the present road was opened in 1833, "with post horses and every accommodation the public could wish". The development of the village of Carlops is described under Route 10, and the associations of Allan Ramsay's *Gentle Shepherd* with Newhall and Habbie's Howe under Route 9. The Old Biggar Road which, since Dolphinton, has been running an almost parallel course at some distance on the left, unites with the modern road through Carlops, but just north of the Esk takes its own line again and parts of it can be seen almost to Silverburn. Rullion Green and the Martyrs'

Monument, beyond a field on the left as the road begins the descent to Flotterstone, are described under Route 2, as is also R. L. Stevenson's links with Glencorse Old Kirk on the right, and Sir Walter Scott's associations with Woodhouselee. An alternative route from West Linton, providing excellent views of the Pentlands, is by the road branching off in the village, opposite the Linton Hotel in Main Street, and running north-east across Harlaw Muir and Auchencorth Moss to Penicuik, and so on to join the Biggar Road at Hillend or go directly into town by Liberton.

19. Wild Life : Ornithology

THE rich variety of wildlife found in the Pentlands reflects the diversity of habitats within the area. They range through rough and improved grassland to heather moor, including both coniferous and deciduous woodland and large expanses of open water.

Most of the area is semi-natural owing to various land use activities such as de-forestation, drainage, grazing, fertilising and heather burning. Habitats have been drastically altered by these techniques, e.g. marshland has been drained and scrub cleared causing the local extinction of some plants and animals while allowing others to colonize the newly created habitats.

There is a predominance of grassland on the hills composed of mainly Mat Grass with varying cover of Fescues, Bent and Wavy Hair Grass, depending on the extent to which the land has been improved. Skylarks are abundant here and in spring the Lapwing, or Peewit, can be viewed going through its repertoire of noisy acrobatics above its chosen nesting territory.

Heather moor is found on some of the slopes and summits of the Pentland Hills and supports its own typical community of plants and animals. Meadow Pipits are very common here and the occasional Red Grouse is raised by the walker. Brown Hares and Rabbits can be seen and occasionally, on higher ground, the Blue or Mountain Hare which can change their coats in winter to white to merge better with their surroundings. Among the plants to be found here are Ling and Bell Heather, Blaeberry and the little yellow Tormentil which seems at home in almost any type of habitat.

Although trees are to be found growing as high as 1,600 feet on Scald Law, they are wind shaped conifers, usually stunted and we have to move lower down to obtain any decent cover. Woodland is not extensive in the Pentlands, though the remnants of Birch, Rowan, Willow, Hawthorn and Juniper testify that at one time much of the area was well endowed with trees. Today conifers like Scots Pine and European Larch can be found planted in shelter blocks, each with their own community of Goldcrests, Britain's smallest bird, Coal and Blue Tits, Chaffinches and the inevitable Woodpigeon, one of our main agricultural pests. Their platforms of sticks are easily picked out among the branches. Below these trees plants are scarce due to the lack of light but ferns thrive nonetheless.

Scattered patches of Birch and, on the wetter ground, Willows provide Willow Warblers, Chaffinches, Dunnocks, Robins and Wrens with food and nest sites and, in the more open areas, Yellowhammers, Reed Buntings and Linnets thrive. These areas are regularly patrolled by scavengers such as Carrion Crows and Jackdaws, while species of gulls such as Blackheaded, Common and Lesser Black-backed are seldom absent.

One of the birds of prey likely to be encountered is the hovering Kestrel, our commonest falcon which destroys such pests as Shrews, Voles, Fieldmice and other small rodents and includes small birds and insects in its catholic diet.

The creation of reservoirs in the area has had a dramatic effect on improving the variety of wildlife. Their importance is illustrated by the fact that Threipmuir Reservoir is classed as a Site of Special Scientific Interest and has a Class I category (of national importance). Between the perimeter fence and the open water at Threipmuir no less than seventy-seven species of plants have been identified.

From the bridge over Threipmuir, 220 acres of open water and an excellent breeding marsh, one can observe to great advantage the resident bird populations. The magnificent Great Crested Grebe can be watched diving under the surface in search of small frogs, newts and fish. More commonly, the Coots, Moorhens, Tufted and Mallard Ducks can be viewed as well as Mute Swans.

It is during the winter months that Threipmuir becomes extremely important as a wildlife refuge. Up to 600 Mallard and 240 Wigeon have been seen and other species include the tiny Teal, Goldeneye, Tufted Duck and the noisy Whooper Swan. Other reservoirs are important too. Cobbinshaw has records of 45 Goldeneye and 60 Tufted Ducks.

The Pentlands, free from the distraction of coastal wild-fowlers, is an important area for roosting geese. A chain of roosts has been identified. Cobbinshaw has as many as 2,000 Pink-Footed Geese and Harperrig 650 Greylags, adding spice to the wildness of a winter stroll. At present, the number of Greylag Geese in the Moorfoots and Pentlands has been estimated at 1,500 with the number of Pink-Footed being put at 5,000.

But still we have not exhausted the wildlife interests in the area. Around Habbies Howe, for example, an important community of calcicole (chalk-loving) plants is situated, meriting being classified as an S.S.S.I. (In all, 44 species have been identified). Entirely different again is the plant community found on Kitchen Moss, a relatively undisturbed peat area on which research has been done by a team from Edinburgh University. Mosses, heaths, grasses and wet-loving plants are well represented here.

Amongst the mammals, Badger, Fox and Roe Deer, although not often seen by the casual visitor, are all resident within the Pentland Hills area. More often seen are the predatory Weasels and Stoats. A walk in the Pentlands thus affords the chance to see a wide variety of plants and animals, which despite changes in land use, have retained a strong foothold in this diverse part of the country.

Ornithology

The Pentlands, although not boasting any particularly rare species, possess a wide variety of bird-life. The high tops and moorlands have been managed specifically for Red Grouse production; Meadow Pipits also enjoy these heathery areas. Lower down, the arable areas are populated by such typical farm-land birds as Skylarks and Lapwing.

The reservoirs have increased the diversity of bird-life in the hills: Great Crested and Little Grebes now nest regularly and thousands of Geese use these open stretches of water as roosting-sites in the winter. Recent plantings by the Forestry Commission have further diversified the Pentlands scene: Goldcrests and Coal Tits thrive here, and Sparrowhawks and Short-eared Owls are showing a welcome increase.

The following list of birds include passage migrants and winter visitors, as well as the breeding species, to be found in the Pentland Hills.

Little Grebe
Great Crested Grebe
Fulmar
Cormorant
Heron
Greylag Goose
Pink-footed Goose
Mute Swan
Whooper Swan
Mallard
Teal
Wigeon
Pochard
Tufted Duck
Goldeneye
Red-breasted Merganser
Goosander
Sparrowhawk
Hen Harrier
Merlin
Kestrel
Black-headed Gull
Common Tern
Wood Pigeon

Red Grouse
Black Grouse
Partridge
Pheasant
Moorhen
Coot
Oystercatcher
Ringed Plover
Golden Plover
Lapwing
Dunlin
Redshank
Greenshank
Common Sandpiper
Curlew
Woodcock
Snipe
Great Black-backed Gull
Lesser Black-backed Gull
Herring Gull
Common Gull
Spotted Flycatcher
Whinchat
Stonechat

Stock Dove
Collared Dove
Cuckoo
Barn Owl
Long-eared Owl
Short-eared Owl
Tawny Owl
Swift
Green Woodpecker
Great Spotted Woodpecker
Skylark
Sand Martin
House Martin
Swallow
Tree Pipit
Meadow Pipit
Grey Wagtail
Pied Wagtail
Great Grey Shrike
Dipper
Wren
Dunnock
Grasshopper Warbler
Sedge Warbler
Garden Warbler
Blackcap
Whitethroat
Willow Warbler
Chiff-chaff
Wood Warbler
Goldcrest
Wheatear
Redstart
Robin
Fieldfare
Ring Ouzel
Blackbird
Redwing
Song Thrush
Mistle Thrush
Long-tailed Tit
Coal Tit
Blue Tit
Great Tit
Treecreeper
Corn Bunting
Yellowhammer
Reed Bunting
Chaffinch
Brambling
Greenfinch
Goldfinch
Linnet
Redpoll
Bullfinch
House Sparrow
Tree Sparrow
Starling
Magpie
Jackdaw
Rook
Carrion Crow

20. Geology of the Pentland Hills

At three successive periods during Palaeozoic times (570–225 million years) the crust of the earth in the neighbourhood of Edinburgh was affected by movements of compression which resulted in the production of a series of great folds, the axes of which lay to the north-east and south-west. The range of the Pentland Hills, which forms the dominating topographical feature, follows the same general direction, coinciding in the main with the trend of a great anticline or arch belonging to the last of the three periods of crustal movement. The core of the denuded fold is occupied by older rocks of Silurian age, and these are flanked in turn by strata belonging to the Old Red Sandstone and Carboniferous formations.

Succession of Rocks in the Pentland Hills

Period	Approximate Age in Millions of Years	Representative Rocks in the Pentland Hills Area
Recent	12,000 years	meltwater channels etc.
Pleistocene	2 m. years	"the ice age"—boulder clay etc.
....	....	thousands of feet of rock worn away since Carboniferous times
Lower Carboniferous	350–330 m. years	calciferous sandstone
Upper Old Red Sandstone Lower Old Red Sandstone	400–350 m. years	sandstones, conglomerates, volcanic lavas and tuffs.
Silurian	450–400 m. years	shales and sandstones

The ancient Silurian core of the Pentland Hills is exposed in only three places: near the headwaters of the Lyne and the North Esk, at Bavelaw Castle and at Loganlee. The rocks can generally be described as a succession of marine shales interbedded with sandstone, the whole series being compressed and highly folded. It is in these rocks that the famous "Eurypterid" and starfish beds occur, although other marine fossils can more easily be found in the Lyne Water and its tributaries.

The rocks of the succeeding period, the Old Red Sandstone, have contributed most to the present structure and scenery of the Pentland Hills. Following the close of the Silurian period, a long period of denudation resulted in the removal of thousands of feet of strata. It was on this worn-down, highly folded, platform that a thick series of coarse conglomerates and sandstones were deposited, much of the material deriving from the high ground of the Southern Uplands. The conglomerates can best be seen in the area of Habbie's Howe.

At the same time as these rocks were being laid down, volcanic activity was on the increase, apparently centred somewhere immediately to the north of the Pentland Hills. An extraordinary series of alternating lavas and tuffs (volcanic ash) was deposited which can be classified into four main groups, all easily recognised in the field:

1. The more basic rocks, andesites and basalts, are richly charged with iron oxides, mainly haematite. Consequently, the screes and weathered outcrops possess a characteristic dark red colour.
2. The rhyolitic types are silicified and their flinty character and the pale colour of the scree material afford a sure means of identification.
3. The lavas of intermediate composition have decomposed to "claystones", usually grey, lilac or buff in colour.
4. The tuffs or volcanic ash, are pale in colour and contain distinct fragments of other rock.

These volcanic rocks, together with a number of minor intrusions, such as the Felsite of Black Hill, occupy most of the Pentland Hills north of West Kip. Being tougher and more resilient than the rocks which eventually covered them, they have withstood the forces of denudation and remain as a group of picturesque hills, which add greatly to the beauty of the Central Valley of Scotland.

The red sandstone, cornstone and marls of the Upper Old Red Sandstone system rest with complete unconformity on all the earlier rocks, including the Silurian. It is clear that there was a prolonged period of denudation between the folding of the Lower and the deposition of the Upper Old Red Sandstone which removed thousands of feet of strata and eventually exposed the core rocks.

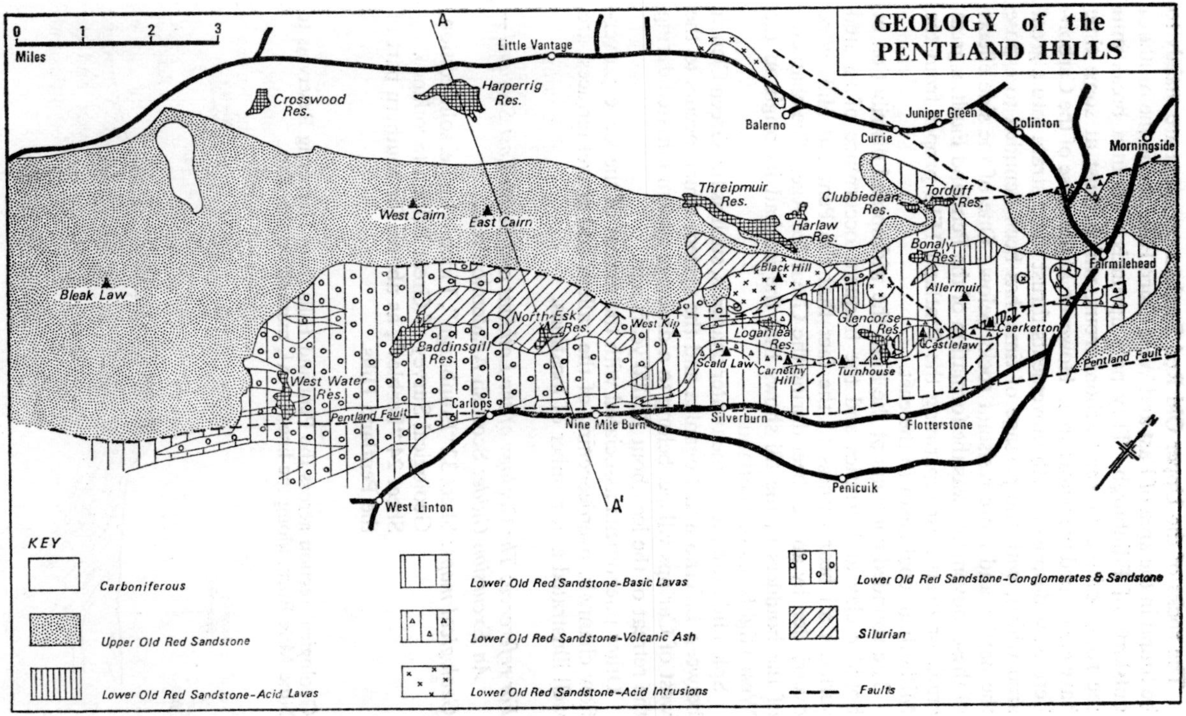

GEOLOGY of the PENTLAND HILLS
0
1
2
3
Miles
A
A'
Little Vantage
Crosswood Res.
Harperrig Res.
Balerno
Currie
Juniper Green
Colinton
Morningside
Threipmuir Res.
Clubbiedean Res.
Torduff Res.
Harlaw Res.
Bonaly Res.
Fairmilehead
West Cairn
East Cairn
Bleak Law
Black Hill
Allermuir
North Esk Res.
West Kip
Loganlea Res.
Glencorse Res.
Castlelaw
Caerketton
Baddinsgill Res.
Scald Law
Carnethy Hill
Turnhouse
West Water Res.
Pentland Fault
Carlops
Nine Mile Burn
Silverburn
Flotterstone
Penicuik
West Linton
N
KEY
Carboniferous
Upper Old Red Sandstone
Lower Old Red Sandstone-Acid Lavas
Lower Old Red Sandstone-Basic Lavas
Lower Old Red Sandstone-Volcanic Ash
Lower Old Red Sandstone-Acid Intrusions
Lower Old Red Sandstone-Conglomerates & Sandstone
Silurian
Faults

The rocks of the Upper Old Red Sandstone system are mainly to be found in the area of East and West Cairn Hills and in the southern outskirts of Edinburgh. They pass upwards without a break into the rocks of the Lower Carboniferous, which must at some time have enveloped the whole area. However, at the close of the Carboniferous, widespread earth movements thrust those strata into a great arch which, with the passage of time, has been denuded to expose the harder and more resistant rocks below. One of the side effects of these movements was the formation of the Pentland Fault, a great crack or overthrust separating the Pentland Hills proper from the Midlothian coal basin to the east.

The rounded contours of the hills, the widespread distribution of boulder clay and erratics and the frequent occurrence of striated surfaces all bear witness to the fact that the Pentland Hills were overridden by an ice sheet during the Great Ice Age. The character of the boulders in the till shows that the ice had its origin in the West Highlands of Scotland.

Splendid examples of meltwater channels, such as the Green Cleuch between Balerno and Loganlea and the system which occurs to the west of Carlops village, belong to a drainage system initiated during the retreat of the ice about 12,000 years ago.

Other phenomena associated with the retreat of the ice, e.g. overflow channels, overdeepening of the valleys and gravel terraces, are well illustrated at a number of locations.

For reference: The Geology of the Lothians and South East Scotland—An Excursion Guide: Scottish Academic Press.

Geological maps: Sheet 32 "Edinburgh", 1 inch = 1 mile, solid edition, Geological Survey of Great Britain (Scotland).
Sheet 24 "Peebles", as above, for southern part of the Pentland Hills.

Geological section across the Pentland Hills from Harperrig Reservoir to Nine Mile Burn, along the line A—A¹, marked on the plan.

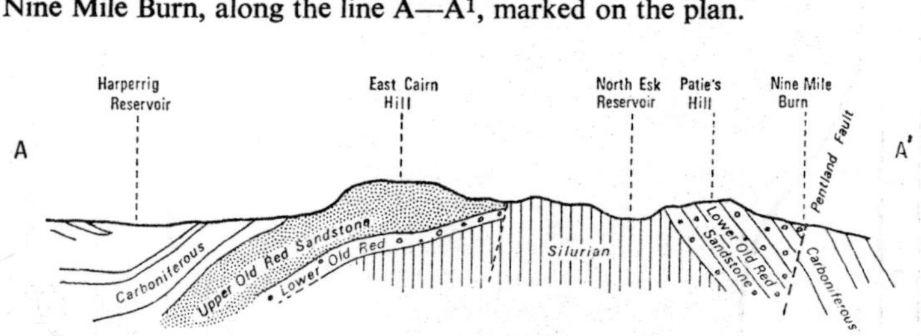

21. Bibliography: a Selection

W.A.S., *The Pentland Hills, their Paths and Passes.*

Grant, Will, *The Call of the Pentlands.*

Grant, Will, *Pentland Days and Country Ways.*

Reith, George M., *The Breezy Pentlands.*

Anderson, William, *The Pentland Hills.*

Terry, C. S., *The Pentland Rising and Rullion Green.*

Sonntag, C. O., *Pocket Flora of Edinburgh and District.*

Geddie, John, *The Water of Leith from Source to Sea.*

Warrender, Margaret, *Walks near Edinburgh.*

Tweedie, John, and Jones, Cyril: *Our District—Currie and Ratho.*

Tweedie, John, *A Water of Leith Walk 1974.*

Ratcliffe Barnett, T., *Border Byways and Lothian Lore.*

Wilson, J. J., *Annals of Penicuik.*

Jackson, James, *Account of the Parish of Penicuik.*

Statistical Account; Colinton, Currie, Penicuik, West Linton parishes.

Miller, Hugh, *Edinburgh and its Neighbourhood.*

Colston, James, *Edinburgh and District Water Supply.*

Lauder, Sir T. Dick, *Scottish Rivers.*

Murray, Thomas, *Biographical Annals of the Parish of Colinton.*

Shankie, David, *The Parish of Colinton.*

Reid, Alan, *West Lothian and Neighbourhood.*

M'Gibbon and Ross, *Castellated and Domestic Architecture of Scotland.*

Small, John, LL.D., *Castles and Mansions of the Lothians.*

Passages in the Lives of Helen Alexander and James Currie of Pentland.

Cowan, Charles, *Reminiscences. Privately printed. Memoirs of the Life of Sir John Clerk of Penicuik.*

Bonnar, T., *Memoir of George Meikle Kemp.*

Burgon, J. W., *Memoir of Patrick Fraser Tytler.*

The Woodhouselee MS. Edited by C. E. S. Chambers.

Cockburn, Lord, *Memorials.*

Cockburn, Lord, *Journal.*

Inglis, J. A., *The Family of Inglis of Auchendinny and Redhall.*

Morrison, William, *Johnston of Warriston.*

Lawlor, H. C., *A History of the Family of Cairns.*

Somerville, James, *The Baronial House of Somerville.*

Brown, John, M.D., *Horae Subsecivae. 1st Series.*

Stevenson, R. L., *The Pentland Rising.*

Stevenson, R. L., *Memories and Portraits.*

Stevenson, R. L., *Edinburgh—Picturesque Notes.*
Transactions of the Edinburgh Architectural Association. Vol. 3 (*for Bavelaw and St. Catherine's*).
Proceedings of Society of Antiquaries. Vol. 33 for Cross at Monks Rig; Vol. 40 for Graves on Island, North Esk Reservoir; Vol. 41 for Pentland Churchyard.
Douglas, W. S., *Cromwell's Scotch Campaigns, 1650–51.*
Buchan, J. W., *History of Peeblesshire. 3 vols.*
Pennecuik, Alexander, *A Description of Tweeddale.*
Historical Monuments Commission: *Midlothian. Peeblesshire.*

Poetry and Fiction

The Gentle Shepherd, with Illustrations of the Scenery. (Evidently by R. D. C. Brown of Newhall). With thirteen engravings of the scenery and portrait of Allan Ramsay.
Brown, R. D. C., Advocate, of Newhall and Carlops, *The Historical Scottish Village, and other Pastorals of Linton Green, or The Third Market Day in June 1685; Carlops Green in 1793, etc.*
Sanderson, R., *Frae the Lyne Valley* (*Poems and Sketches*).
Campbell, Alexander, *Poems.*
Ballads and Songs by David Mallet. Edited by F. Dinsdale.
Thomson, James, *Poems in the Scottish Dialect.*
Ballantine, James, *Poems.*
Ballantine, James, *The Miller of Deanhaugh.*
Grant, James, *Harry Ogilvie.*
Stevenson, R. L., *Weir of Hermiston.*
Stevenson, R. L., *St. Ives.*
Buchan, John, *John Burnet of Barns.*
Buchan, John, *The Moon Endureth.* (Contains poem, *From the Pentlands, looking North and South*).
Buchan, John, *Salute to Adventurers.*
Moncrieff, R. H., *The Martyr Shepherd.*
Orr, Christine, *Kate Curlew.*
Hamilton, Elizabeth, *The Cottagers of Glenburnie.*

The Scottish Rights of Way Society Limited

For the past century and a quarter the Society has been active in the preservation and defence of rights of way in Scotland and it is due to the Society's vigilance that many routes which would otherwise have been lost forever are today open to the public.

The Society is an independent body, not officially sponsored or assisted financially, but entirely dependent on the support of its members. Membership is open to all for a small annual subscription. For further information, terms of membership and form of application apply to The Secretary, 28 Rutland Square, Edinburgh, EH1 2BW.

22. Index